Native Reenacting Made Easy

How to Portray an Eastern Woodland Warrior

Axehead
Publishing

Michael L. Pitzer

Michael L. Pitzer

Native Reenacting Made Easy, How to Portray an Eastern Woodland Warrior

Copyright © 2009 Michael L. Pitzer. All rights reserved, including the right to reproduce this book, or portions thereof, in any form. No part of this text may be reproduced, transmitted, downloaded, decompiled, reverse engineered, or stored in or introduced into any information storage and retrieval system, in any form or by any means, whether electronic or mechanical without the express written permission of the author. The scanning, uploading, and distribution of this book via the Internet or via any other means without the permission of the publisher is illegal and punishable by law. Please purchase only authorized electronic editions, and do not participate in or encourage electronic piracy of copyrighted materials. The publisher does not have any control over and does not assume any responsibility for author or third-party websites or their content.

Cover Design: Michael L. Pitzer
Front cover photograph taken by Graphic Enterprises.

Book and eBook Published and Distributed by: Axehead Publishing, LLC www.axeheadpublishing.com
ISBN 978-0-9819975-3-7

Native Reenacting Made Easy

Contents

Preface – Note to Readers...9
Introduction...11
Chapter One..13
Creating Your Persona...13
Chapter Two..21
Shawnee Language Primer..21
Chapter Three..47
Leggings and Breechclouts..47
Chapter Four...57
Moccasins (M'ki-thai-nah)..57
Chapter Five..69
Trade Shirts (Peleneca)...69
Chapter Six...79
Bags (Posan) & Accessories..79
Chapter Seven...91
Paint & Scalplocks..91
Chapter Eight..103
Weapons..103
Chapter Nine...117
Homemade Gunpowder (Macate)...................................117
Appendix A...135
18th Century Documentation..135
Examples of 18th Century Art..150
Appendix B...157
Resources 157
Bibliography...162
HOW TO ORDER..165

Michael L. Pitzer

Dedication

To my loving wife Allison, without whose friendship, patience and encouragement this book would not have been possible. This book is also dedicated to my two wonderful sons, Dakota and Zane. Both have cheerfully endured many trips to historical sites and listened to their dad ramble about how cool it must have been to have lived 250 years ago.

For my remaining family & friends not mentioned by name, you know who you are. I love all of you very much and thanks for the words of encouragement along the way.

Acknowledgments

I would like to thank my good friend Stephen W. Thomas for introducing me to this world so many years ago. He and I have shared some good times discussing history, building rifles and hunting. When first introduced to the flintlock, Steve and I worked at a State Prison and he made me promise to never utter the words "smoke pole" at work for fear of people getting the wrong idea about us. Thanks for teaching a greenhorn how to properly discuss his smoke pole in public. I also want to thank my friend and mentor, A. Denzil Blevins for the positive impact that his friendship has had on my life.

In addition, I thank the following people; Jim & Kathy Cummings of Graphic Enterprises for the use of all of their wonderful photographs, Wallace Gusler for inspiring me to build my first flintlock (you made it look so easy), Jim Wright for answering my endless barrage of questions with such kindness, Michael Lea for bailing me out of my rifle building screw ups, Larry McQuown, Jesse Mudd, Jim Green, and Michael Fields for making me feel like family during my first native event, Dr. R. Michael Abram for explaining the importance of using historically accurate research material, and finally Laura Redish and Orrin Lewis for allowing me to reprint their research on the Shawnee language.

Michael L. Pitzer

About the Author

Michael L. Pitzer is a historian, educator and writer. He developed an appreciation for history and native culture at a very early age and has spent countless hours studying indigenous cultures of North America, traveling to museums and visiting historical sites. Michael holds a Master of Science in Managing Information Technology, Summa Cum Laude from Sullivan University and an Occupational Training Certificate from the University of Louisville. In addition, he has taught for local colleges and public high schools in Louisville, Kentucky. Prior to teaching, the author worked in the public sector as an emergency medical technician, state law enforcement officer and adjunct academy instructor for the Commonwealth of Kentucky.

Native Reenacting Made Easy

Warning & Disclaimer

Some of the processes depicted in this book are extremely dangerous. It is not the intent of the author, publisher or distributors of this book to encourage readers to attempt any of these processes without proper professional supervision and or training. Attempting to do so could result in death or serious physical injury to you or people in your vicinity. The author, publisher and distributors of this book disclaim any liability from damages or injuries of any type that may result from the use or misuse of information contained within this book. Some things mentioned here may be illegal to manufacture in your city, county, state, or country. It is your responsibility to check and comply with all laws that apply to you. This book is for information purposes only.

Michael L. Pitzer

"We know our lands have now become more valuable. The white people think we do not know their value; but we know that the land is everlasting, and the few goods we receive for it are soon worn out and gone."

Canassatego, Mingo

Native Reenacting Made Easy

Preface – Note to Readers

Throughout this book, you will notice that both of the terms "Native" and "Indian" are used to refer to the indigenous cultures that inhabited the North Eastern region of North America. To some, the term Native American is considered offensive because it is viewed as a historically oppressive government telling indigenous people what they should call themselves. To others, the term Indian is equally offensive because it perpetuates European ignorance as to which continent they had landed on.

I do not want to get into the debate about which term is politically correct because I feel that this book is geared toward respectfully portraying a very noble culture rather than labeling it. I can see arguments from both sides; therefore I want to avoid labeling anyone in a derogatory manner. I believe that the Canadians have circumvented this whole debate by simply referring to their indigenous cultures as the "first nations" or "aboriginal peoples". Maybe we could learn something from our Northern neighbors.

Michael L. Pitzer

Caption on Artwork Reads: "The Indians delivering up the English captives to Colonel Bouquet", 1766. Originally published in William Smith, An historical account of the expedition against the Ohio Indians in the year 1764.

Introduction

If you are considering becoming a living history interpreter who portrays an Eastern woodland warrior, then this book is for you. In it, you will find valuable resources and tips that you won't find elsewhere.

Many interpreters earn their "Reenactment PhD" from the school of "Hard Knocks". This is an unpleasant and frustrating way to learn a new hobby and if you are like most, you can't afford to make costly mistakes by buying the wrong gear. The guidance provided in this book will save you time, money, effort and embarrassment by showing you how to do it right the first time.

I have spent the past eight years researching Colonial American history and the white and native interaction of the period. I am just now beginning to realize how much I still don't know about the subject. My first interpretations were not pretty, in fact I am too embarrassed to even show the pictures to anyone remotely knowledgeable. These failures aided me in pinpointing stumbling blocks that can frustrate a novice into giving up before they even get started. In the following pages, I will simplify the initial stages of pulling together a realistic portrayal of an Eastern woodland warrior that you can be proud of. Have fun and enjoy this rewarding hobby.

Michael L. Pitzer

"A single twig breaks, but the bundle of twigs is strong."

Tecumseh, Shawnee

Chapter One
Creating Your Persona

Are you up to the challenge?

Have you ever thought to yourself that becoming a reenactor might be fun? Most people never take the plunge for fear that they might look foolish. Everyone has to start somewhere and by reading this book you have indicated that you are not afraid to learn something new in order to avoid making common novice mistakes. In the world of native interpretations, the willingness to listen to others and learn from mistakes is all that is required to join the native interpretation extended family.

Most native living history groups welcome new reenactors with open arms. These days, finding individuals willing to make the level of commitment necessary to do a good native portrayal is extremely difficult. Good native living history interpretations require shaving your head and painting your body. This is just too much commitment for a hobby they participate in just a few times per year. If you are up to the challenge of doing it right, your fellow hobbyists will mentor and even help outfit you until you can gradually create your own kit (gear). Probably the most important advice I can give you is to thoroughly research the people and time period you are interested in portraying.

Michael L. Pitzer

By taking this extra step you will be creating a historically sound persona or the acting role that you will assume while in costume. Your persona can be based on a real individual or a figment of your imagination that could have lived during your period of interest. Determine what type of person you are interested in portraying rather than basing it on a specific person. This will allow you more freedom in your interpretation.

In addition, for your living history interpretation to be believable, you select a persona that has some personal significance to you. For example, you might discover that your seventh great grandfather was the product of an Indian captivity. Your persona could be loosely based on the life of your ancestor. Having a vested interest in the research will help in creating a more believable persona.

Raid on Martin's Station, 2005 by Graphic Enterprises

Native Reenacting Made Easy

Three Easy Steps to Creating a Persona

Step #1 - Choose a narrow or specific time period & location. This stops you from making costly mistakes when buying gear for your living history interpretation. Just as it does today, lifestyles of natives differed greatly depending upon the geographical location of the tribe. If you were planning to portray an 18th century Iroquois warrior you would not want to buy or make side seam leggings because the Iroquois wore center seam. Narrowing the tribe and time frame will avoid making costly gear purchases that are inappropriate for the era or type of person you wish to portray.

Step #2 - Find an organization that shares your commitment to accurate portrayals. The closer to your home, the more likely you will attend club functions and talk to fellow members. These groups can be a big help in finding the best gear for your money and guiding you past newbie gotchas. The camaraderie will help keep you involved. Over time, fellow interpreters will also become like an adopted family to you.

Step #3 - Find primary documentation written or painted during your era and that depicts your particular tribe of interest. This means finding a local historical society to research through. Be willing to spend some long hours researching data from primary sources before finalizing the essence of your persona. I have included examples of

Michael L. Pitzer

18th century primary sources at the end of this chapter. Learn everything you can about the character such as the way they dressed, ate, spoke, their cultural & religious beliefs, social interactions, etc. Immerse yourself in the era by reading primary source document related to the type of person you've chosen to portray you can find. Ask yourself some questions such as;

- What was this person's lifestyle?
- Was this person a hunter, a trader, a captive, an adoptee, a chief, a warrior, or a runaway slave?
- What was this person's social status, ethnic background?
- Where, when, and how did they live?
- What were core societal beliefs that would have caused behaviors such as mutilating the bodies of the dead enemies?
- What language did they speak and why?
- Who were their traditional enemies and allies? (Odom, 2004)

Native Reenacting Made Easy

Tips for Creating Memorable Authenticity

Adapted from an Internet Article by Alan Gutchess

Document first! - Create only after making sure that you have found acceptable documentation derived from era accounts, illustrations or surviving objects. You want first person accounts (diaries, journals, military or other governmental reports). Look for writings by early traders, missionaries, soldiers, native captives and other individuals who may have met and documented native peoples during the time period you portray. A notebook of all documentation should then be retained. I am not suggesting that you become a thread counter unless that is your ultimate goal. However, I am saying that historical basis should be taken into account when creating items for living history interpretations.

Dare to be average! - Creating a persona should mean that if you were to travel back to your era of interest, people would not see you as out of place, strange or unusual. There were, and always will be freaks or outcasts in any society but this should not be your goal.

Leave the fancy gear for the wannabes! - Native warriors were very practical. They routinely acquired gear from fallen enemies and picked up plunder from successful raids. However, the truth is that most would have made or traded for their gear. In the 18th century, the white man was not known for trading the finest wares to the Indians. Save your money and buy practical gear that you know is well documented. Remember, the goal of your portrayal is reality, not a Hollywood rendition.

Don't wear it because everyone else does! - Nothing is more disappointing to knowledgeable spectators than seeing inappropriate attire at a period event. You must be willing to deviate from the pack when it is appropriate to do so. Admittedly, some items are not and will not ever be fully documented. In those situations, try to find something similar based on documentation from another group in that same time period. If someone were to study the 21st century in the year 2209 they probably wouldn't find sufficient documentation on how a telephone was dialed because it is considered to be a "common sense" activity. That being said, I am fairly certain that several similarly mundane things have slipped by previous generations for the same reasons.

Accept that you can't make it all yourself! - Somewhere along the line people have gotten the idea that when a pioneer or Indian needed shoes, gun, clothes, powder horn, or any other necessity, they just made it themselves. This is a fairy tale perpetuated by Hollywood. Trades were highly specialized affairs even among the Native tribes. Most tribes had medicine men, soldiers, hunters, craftsmen, etc. Don't ruin an otherwise good interpretation by wearing terribly crafted accessories of your own making.

Native Reenacting Made Easy

If you are talented in a specific area, trade your creations for the crafts of other equally talented reenactors. Bartering is still the best way to get what you need.

Avoid crafts made with synthetic materials! - Artificial sinew, aka waxed nylon thread is the bane of all native reenactors. Use period correct materials to sew stuff together. Synthetic materials have no place among serious hobbyists. People will know you are a greenhorn (or an idiot) if you show up wearing synthetic materials.

As you learn, re-evaluate your kit! - Make corrections to your kit as you mature in the hobby and use your gear. What you think is needed and what experience in the field will teach you will change in time. As you acquire experience and figure out what is not needed, tweak your kit. This is the basis of a movement called experimental archeology.

Have the heart of a teacher! - Remember where you came from. Help others in this hobby by sharing knowledge freely. It is perfectly acceptable to write articles, books, and create Internet web sites to share your expertise. Sell the information or give it away, but do not use it to "one up" others! We all benefit from the free exchange of information.

Michael L. Pitzer

"We have beaten the enemy every time; we cannot expect the same good fortune always to attend us. The Americans are now led by a chief who never sleeps. In spite of the watchfulness of our braves, we have never been able to surprise him. There is something that whispers to me that it would be prudent to listen to offers of peace."

Little Turtle, Miami

Native Reenacting Made Easy

Chapter Two
Shawnee Language Primer

Shawnee is the language and it belongs to the Algonquian family of languages. This is very similar to German being the language spoken in Germany while Germanic language dialects are spoken in the Netherlands, Iceland and other countries. The Algonquian Indian languages are closely related to Ojibwe. In fact, speakers of both can roughly understand each other in a manner similar to the way that Spanish and Italian speakers of Europe can get the gist of what is being said between the two languages. Somewhere along the line, people started saying that Algonquin is somehow related to Ancient Egyptian, Hebrew, or other Semitic languages. The truth of the matter is that people have made up words in Algonquin and asserted that they are similar in meaning and spelling to Hebrew words. This is simply NOT true. I will help debunk this myth by showing numbers one through five in Hebrew and Algonquin. You can judge whether or not they sound or look similar (Redish & Lewis, 1998-2008).

English	**Hebrew**	**Algonquin**
One	Echad	Pejig
Two	Shtayim	Nìj
Three	Shalosh	Niswi
Four	Arba	New
Five	Chamesh	Nànan

Michael L. Pitzer

What tribes were Algonquin?

Algonquian tribes of the New England area include Micmac, Passamaquoddy, Abenaki, Pennacook, Massachusett, Nipmuck, Pocomtuc, Wampanoag, Nauset, Sakonnet, Narragansett, Niantic, Mohegan, Pequot, Montauk, Wappinger and Mahican Stockbridge.

The Midwest Algonquin tribes consisted of the Shawnee, Illiniwek, Kickapoo, Menominee, Miami, Sac and Fox.

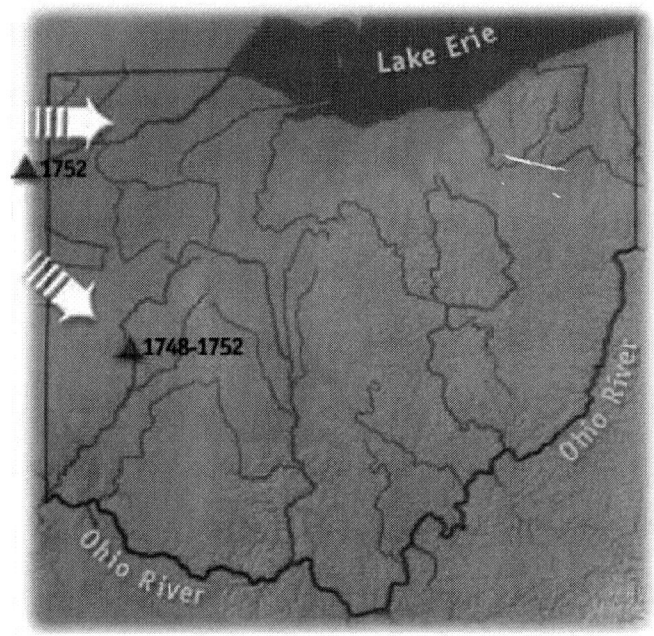

Miami Tribal movement map by year

Native Reenacting Made Easy

The mid and south-Atlantic were home to the Powhatan, Lumbee, Nanticoke and Lenape. The Lenape moved into Ohio around the mid 18th century (Johnson & Hook, 1990).

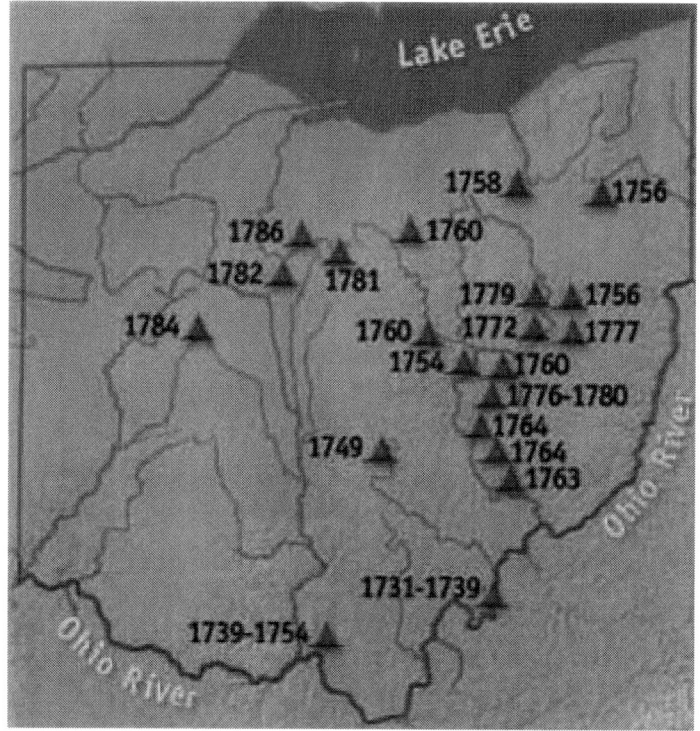

Delaware (Lenape) Tribal movement map by year

Michael L. Pitzer

The Shawnee Dialect

The Shawnee dialect of the Algonquian family of languages is not well documented. Fortunately, other closely related Algonquian languages are very well documented and share commonalities. Of these, Lenape or Delaware is the best known due to the amount of time spent with early Moravian missionaries working to Christianize them. The early missionaries translated prayers into Lenape and created written records that survive to this day (Wenning, 2000). The Lenape, Shawnee as well as other Algonquins could communicate with relative ease. This is similar to the way Kentuckians and New Yorkers communicate. Despite pronouncing words differently, using different slang they retain the ability to fully understand each other. The map shows the movement of the Lenape which would lead a reasonable person to believe that there must have been frequent contact and interaction with other Algonquin tribes. In fact, the Shawnee and Delaware frequently camped together, thus strengthening the claim that they could communicate effectively (Redish & Lewis, 1998-2008).

Much of the surviving Shawnee language specimen can be traced to two compilations by military officers that served in the areas occupied by the Shawnee; Colonel John Johnson and Major Ebenezer Denny. Both men documented the spoken words and phrases of the Shawnee, Delaware and Wyandott tribes.

Native Reenacting Made Easy

Shawnee Pronunciation Guide

Used with permission from Laura Redish

Vowels

Character:	How To Pronounce It:
a	Like the a in father or the a in what.
aa	Like the a in father, only held longer.
e	Like the a in gate or the e in get.
ee	Like the a in gate, only held longer.
i	Like the ee in seek or the i in sick.
ii	Like the ee in see, only held longer.
o	Like the o in rode or the u in rude.
oo	Like the o in rode, only held longer.

Consonants

Character:	How To Pronounce It:
č	Like ch in char or j in jar
h	Like h in hay.
k	Like the k in skate or g in gate.
m	Like m in English moon.
n	Like n in English night.
p	Like the p in spill or b in bill.
š	Like sh in shy or s in pleasure.
t	Like the t in sty or d in die.
θ	Like th in thin or th in this.
w	Like w in English way.
y	Like y in English yes.
ʼ	A pause sound, like the word "uh-oh."

Michael L. Pitzer

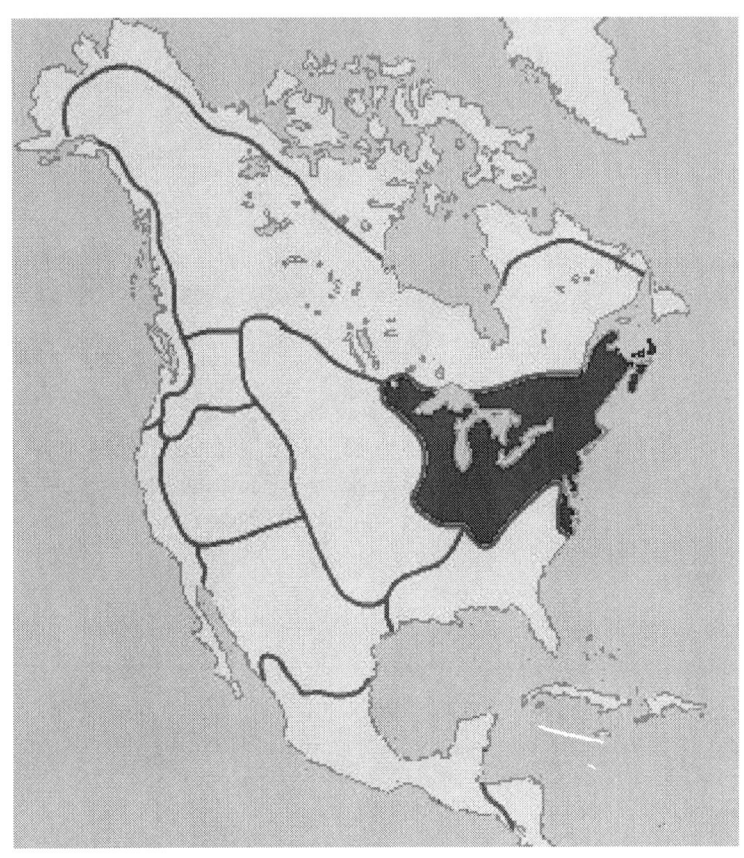

Map showing the geographic region where Algonquian languages were spoken

Native Reenacting Made Easy

Consonant Voicing and Aspiration

In Shawnee, all consonants are unaspirated (pronounced without a breath of air). The Shawnee letter k, for example, is always pronounced like the soft "k" in the English word "skill" rather than the hard "k" in the English word "kill." (If you're uncertain about the difference, place your fingers in front of your mouth and say "kill," then "skill." You can feel more air puffing out of your mouth with the aspirated "k" in "kill" than the unaspirated "k" in "skill"). English k is sometimes aspirated and sometimes not, but Shawnee k never is. Just the opposite from English, Shawnee consonants are sometimes voiced (pronounced with the vocal chords vibrating) and other times unvoiced. (You can feel the difference in English by placing your fingers on your voice box and pronouncing the words "utter" and "udder").

Shawnee t is sometimes voiced and sometimes not, but English t never is. For some Shawnee speakers, voicing is used in a consistent way. Those speakers pronounce consonants as unvoiced except between two vowels or after an n or m. Other Shawnee speakers will pronounce the same word with a voiced consonant one minute, and with an unvoiced consonant the next minute. All these Shawnee speakers can understand each other easily. Voicing is not very important to the Shawnee language. It is much more important to remember not to aspirate consonants the way you would in English.

Michael L. Pitzer

Stress

Shawnee has less pronounced word stress than English does. In English, unstressed vowels are often weakened to schwas, which makes the stress sound very strong. (An example of this is the word "rebel." When "rebel" is a noun, the stress is on the first syllable and the word is pronounced REH-bal. When "rebel" is a verb, the stress is on the second syllable and the word is pronounced ra-BELL.) But in Shawnee, all vowels are pronounced the same regardless of stress. If you weaken an unstressed vowel you will often change the meaning of the word, so be careful not to do this! Although stress is less pronounced than it is in English, it is still present. Generally speaking, the stress is on the last syllable of a Shawnee word.

Animate & Inanimate Nouns

Some adjectives have two or three different forms in Shawnee--for example, "red" is translated as mškwa in Shawnee, but the red rock is mškwawi, and the red bird is mškwaawiθi. That's because there is a distinction in Shawnee between animate and inanimate nouns. If you're familiar with a European language like Spanish or French, nouns in those languages are divided by gender. In those European languages, adjectives describing masculine and feminine nouns have different endings.

Native Reenacting Made Easy

So if you want to use the word "old" to describe a man in Spanish, you say viejo, but if you want to describe a woman, you say vieja. For men and women, this is easy to remember, but for other nouns, you just have to remember their grammatical gender. In Algonquian languages like Shawnee, you use the same adjective and verb forms regardless of whether the subject is male or female. Instead, there are different word forms depending on whether the subject is animate or inanimate. All people and animals are considered animate in Shawnee, but for other nouns, you just have to remember whether they are animate or not. You probably wouldn't be able to guess that "feather" is animate and "river" is inanimate in Shawnee any more than you would be able to guess that "feather" is feminine and "river" is masculine in Spanish. The third form is a prefix form. So instead of saying wiškiloθa wakanakiθi you could also say waapa-wiškiloθa, white bird. That prefix is the same for both animate and inanimate nouns.

θikun wakanaki	(the rock is white)
wiškiloθa wakanakiθi	(the bird is white)
θikuna wakanaka	(the rocks are white)
wiškiloθaki wakanakiθiki	(the birds are white)
θikun mškwaawi	(the rock is red)
wiškiloθa mškwaawiθi	(the bird is red)
θikuna mškwaawa	(the rocks are red)
wiškiloθaki mškwaawiθiki	(the birds are red)

Michael L. Pitzer

Possession

N- is a Shawnee prefix that means "my." Possessive prefixes can be used with almost any noun in Shawnee. The possessive prefixes are ni-, ki-, or ho- before most nouns that start with consonants, and nit-, kit-, or hot- before most nouns that start with vowels.

haθaya	(a pelt)
nitaθaya	(my pelt)
kitaθaya	(your pelt)
hotaθaya	(their pelt)

However, certain nouns (including most body parts and kinship terms, and some words for personal objects like clothing) have inalienable possession in Algonquian languages like Shawnee. That means you must use a possessive prefix with one of those words. You cannot say *kya, "a mother," or *tooni, "a mouth." It isn't grammatically correct. For these words, the possessive pronouns are slightly different. The prefixes are usually ni-, ki-, and ho- before nouns beginning with a consonant, and n-, k-, and w- before nouns beginning with a vowel. Before nouns beginning with h, the third person possessive prefix is usually not pronounced at all.

*kya	(root noun, not used alone)
nikya	(my mother)
kikya	(your mother)
hokyali	(his or her mother)

Native Reenacting Made Easy

*tooni	(root noun, not used alone)
nitooni	(my mouth)
kitooni	(your mouth)
hotooni	(his or her mouth)

When animate words use the third person form ("his or her"), there is not only a prefix (w-) but also a suffix (-li) at the end of the word. This is not true for inanimate words. Not every Shawnee noun will exactly fit this pattern. Every language, including Shawnee, has irregular words. If you make a mistake, a Shawnee speaker will probably still understand you, just like an English speaker understands a person who says "fighted" instead of "fought."

Raid on Martin's Station, 2008 by Graphic Enterprises

Michael L. Pitzer

Shawnee Dictionary & Phrases

Adapted from "Specimen of Shawanoese & Wyandott, or Huron Language" as Recorded by Col. John Johnston

Conversational Phrases

Hello -Bezon

Good Day -Way-se-gi-se-gi

I am very well -Ni wes hela shamamo

I am Shawnee -Lenawe nilla

We are Shawnee -Sawanwa killa

I speak Shawnee -Ni-sawanwa-towe

I speak English -Ni-wakota ys'asi tekosi-w-aatoweeya

Be quiet! -Nooleewi-a

Be Strong! -Oui-shi-cat-to-oui!

I am well -Ni howesi la-suh muh-muh ulami

Thank you -Neahw

Great Warrior -Psai-wi ne-noth-tu

You are my enemy -Matchele ne tha-tha

Follow! -Pe-e-wah

Throw it away! -Puck-e-ton!

Danger! (warning) -Puck-a-chee

Native Reenacting Made Easy

Basic Speech

Yes -Hahhah

No -Mat-tah

That -La-nah

They -La-neh-ke

This -La-yah-mah

Who? -Nethowwe

My, mine, myself -Ni (Ne)

Body; physical being -Ni-i-yah

I, me -Ni-la

We, us -Ni-la-weh

Many or much -Metchi

He -Yah-ma

Speak (ordered) -Atchmoloh

Boy -Skillewaythetha

Girl -Squithetha

Bad -Mat-ou-oui-sah

Good -Oui-sah

All; everything -Tscha-yah-ki

Go; leave; depart -Wehpeteh

Come, follow -Pe-e-wah

Michael L. Pitzer

Family Relationships

My father -No'tha
Your father -Ko'tha
My mother -Neegah
Mother -Nik-yah
My brother -Ni-je-ni-nuh
(blood)Brother -Jai-nai-nah
My son -Ni-kwith-ehi
My sister -Ni-t-kweem-a
My daughter -Ni-da-ne-thuh
Daughter -Dah-nai-tha
My husband -Ni-da-ne-thuh
Husband -Wahsiu
You are my husband -Ni wahsiu
My wife -Ni-wa
Your wife -Keewa
You are my wife -Ni haw-ku-nah-ga
My grandmother -No'kom'tha
Grandmother -Cocumtha
My grandfather -Ni-me'soom'tha
My friend -Ne-kah-noh

Numbers

One -Negate
Two -Neshwa
Three -Nithese
Four -Newe
Five -Nialinwe
Six -Negotewathe
Seven -Neshwathe
Eight -Sashekswa
Nine -Chakatswa
Ten -Metathwe

Cardinal Directions

East -wa'ta'pethekwi
West -ta'paksimoci
North -wecipepooki
South -yelaawa'kweki

Michael L. Pitzer

The Seasons

Spring -Me-loh-cak-me
Summer -Ni-pai-n'oui
Autumn -Pahcotai
Winter -Paipoun'oui

The Heavens

Earth -Ake
Sky -Menquotwe
Stars and planets -Alagwa
Darkness -Pai-bai-ke-char
Twilight, dusk -Pakesemou
Sun -Kesathwa
Moon -Te-bethto-kish-thoe
Universe -Ya-la-ku-qua-kumi-gigi

Weather Terms

Storm clouds -Pasquawke

Wind -Wishekuanwe

Rain -Gimewane or keawa

Lightning -Papapanawe

Warm -Aquetteta

Snow -Cone

Ice -Ki-pat-te-nui

A fine day -Washekee sheke

Time

Morning -Piaitahcouthamou

Day -Qui-si-qui

Night -Te-beth-ki

Today -E-no-ke-kah-she-ki-ki

Tomorrow -Wahpahkeh

Yesterday -Ulaoco

Michael L. Pitzer

Significant Rivers in Ohio

Ohio -Kis,ke,pi,la
Great Miami -Shi,me,a,mee,sepe
Little Miami -Che,ke,me,amee,sepe
Mad -Athe,ne,sepe
Licking -Ne,pe,pim,me,sepe
Auglaize -Cow,the,na,ke,sepe
Muskingum -Wa,ka,ta,mo,sepe
Sandusky -Po,ta,ke,sepe
Scioto -Sci,on,to
St. Mary's -Ca,ko,the,ke,sepe

Land Terminology

Water -Nipe
Pond -Miskeque
Swamp -Miskekopke
Valley -Ki-kah-ka-mi-ka-tui
Prairie -Tawaskote
Stone or rock -Shequomur

Native Reenacting Made Easy

Descriptive Terms

Man -Elene

Woman -Equiwa

Young -Mai-ah

Handsome -Ulethi

Ugly -Matethi-i-thi

Over; above -Kit-te

Near, close by -Maketchenelu

Small, little -Match-squa-thi

Alive or living -Lenawawe

Dead -Nepwa

Articles of Clothing

Moccasins (Buffalo) -M'ki-thai-nah

Leggings (Buckskin) -Metetawawa

Hat -Petacowa

Shirt -Peleneca

Breechclout -Akotam

Michael L. Pitzer

Body Parts

Face (expression) -E-shi-que-chi

Bone -H'kah-nih

Ear -H'tow-wa-ca

Tooth -Ki-be-tar-leh

Tongue -Ki-lar-ni

Hand or fingers or both -Ki-leh-chi

Arm -Ki-neh-ki

Heart -Ki-te-hi

Mouth -Ki-tor-ni

Nose -Ki-tschar-si

Forehead -Lah-oui-ki-leh

Foot -Nithichi

Head -Oui-i-si

Beard -Quinilu-narolih

Leg -T'karchi

Hair (on the head) -Oui-thai-ah

Native Reenacting Made Easy

Colors

Black -Mkate
White -Waapa
Yellow -Hoθaawa
Red -mškwa
Green -škipaki
Blue -škipaki

Food Terminology

Eat -Oui-then-eluh
Drink -Meneluh
Salt -Nepepimma
Egg -Oua-oui
Meat, flesh -Oui-or-thi
Breadwater (gruel) -Takuwah-nepi
Bottle, flask -Oui-thai-quuc-quoi

Michael L. Pitzer

Weapons & Tools

Tomahawk -Cheketecaca
Bow -Il-le-nah-qui
Flintlock (Gun or Rifle) -Metequa
Knife -Manese
Bulk Lead (Bullet) -Alwe

Plants & Trees

Tree bark -Oulagequi
Pine tree -S'shequoi
Turnips -Openeake
Nut -Pacan
Onions -Shekagosheke
Oak tree -Wahbah-comeshi
Tree -Te-qui
Melons -Usketomake

Miscellaneous Terminology

Run -Memequiluh

Sing; chant -Nacamoloh

Sleep -Ne-pah-loh

Walk -Pamtheloh

Kill -Tsi or Tschi

Soldier -Shemagana

Chief, leader -Okema

Englishman -Englishmanake

Frenchman -Tota

Whiteman (Longhunter) -Shamanese

Blood -Ps'qui

Bury -Nepaka

State of being sick -Aghqueloge

Medicine -Chobeka

Trap -Naquaga

Town -Ou-te-ou-wel

Gossip (death penalty) -Pockvano-madee-way

House -Wigewa

Fire -Scoote

Michael L. Pitzer

Animals

Any bird -Ouiske-lo-tha
Bear -Muga
Beaver -Amaghqua
Bird -Wiskilo'tha
Buffalo -M'thoothwa
Cat -Posetha
Deer -Peshikthe
Dog -Weshe
Duck -Si'sipa
Eagle -Pele'thi
Elk -Waapitti
Fish -Name'tha
Fox -Waakoce'thi
Frog -Toti
Goose -Lika or nika
Horse -M'seewa
Mink -Chaquiweshe
Moose -Moswa
Muskrat -Oshasqua

Native Reenacting Made Easy

Otter -Kitati

Owl -Miyathwe

Panther -Msipesi

Porcupine -Kakwa

Rabbit -Petakine'thi

Raccoon -Etepate

Rattlesnake -Msithwe

Skunk -Sekakwa

Squirrel -Haniwa or anequoi

Swan -Waapehti

Turkey -Pelewa

Water Turtle -Ka'skotelawe

Land Turtle -Skotelawe

Wildcat -Peshewa

Wolf -M'weowa

Wolves -Petweowas

Michael L. Pitzer

"When you arise in the morning, give thanks for the morning light, for your life and strength. Give thanks for your food, and the joy of living. If you see no reason for giving thanks, the fault lies with yourself"

Tecumseh, Shawnee

Chapter Three
Leggings and Breechclouts

Leggings Overview

Most eastern woodland tribes wore some type of leg covering which is generically referred to as a legging. The legging is simply an optional leg cover that is usually worn with a strip of cloth designed to cover the crotch (breechclout). The purpose of the legging is to protect the leg from harsh weather or brush and leggings should not to be confused with pants, they were more like chaps. Each tribe had its own unique decoration style however; material preferences and the patterns were similar for all. The most common materials chosen were either wool or buckskin depending upon the weather and intended purpose of the wearer.

Wool was generally the preferred material for wet or cold weather because it maintained its insulating qualities even when wet. On the other hand, buckskin was better for traversing difficult country where thorns, burrs or heavy underbrush were common due to its ability to protect the leg better. In warmer weather, buckskin also kept the legs cooler and didn't itch as much. When constructing leggings, forget everything you have seen in the movies, Woodland tribes did not wear fringe because it tended to collect ice in cold weather and got hung up in underbrush in warmer climates.

Michael L. Pitzer

The properly styled legging should have about a one half (1/2") to three quarter (3/4") of an inch tab running the length of the leg and should not extend more than a hand width or so above the knee (see below). Generally, 18th century leggings were cut just above the knee because they were made from half of a trade blanket for each legging. (Hartman, Hudson, Lee & Heath, 2000). Wool leggings should fit snugly but not too tight to in order to promote better circulation in cooler weather whereas the buckskin leggings should fit tighter to the leg.

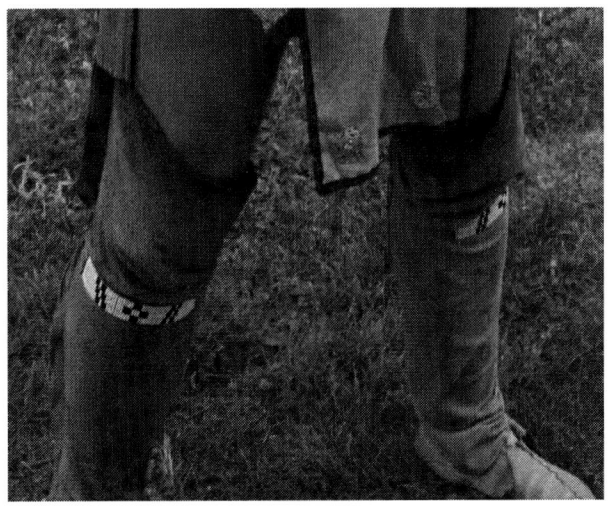

Properly worn skin leggings

Native Reenacting Made Easy

Legging Materials List

- 2.5 Yards of good quality wool. Preferably black, red or dark blue.
- Spool of heavy linen thread. Choose a color close to the wool color.
- Pair of scissors, a plastic tape measure, needles and beeswax.

Legging Construction Details

Step One - Wrap the wool around the leg about one hand width above the knee and mark it when the snugness feels comfortable.

Step Two - Make a single stitch at the mark and place the garment back on your leg to test its fit.

Step Three - Repeat steps one and two at the following points; above the knee, below the knee, at the calf and the ankle.

Step Four - Once the legging fits the leg snugly, sew up the entire seam by connecting the sewn spots using a saddle stitch.

Step Five - Trim the part by the ankle. Leave enough material to keep debris from falling into a moccasin.

Michael L. Pitzer

Step Six - Sew an eighteen inch long by two inch wide strip to the outside edge to tie off to a belt. Repeat for the other leg.

Step Seven - Decorate to taste.

The Saddle Stitch
"The Art of Handsewing Leather" by Al Stohlman (1977)

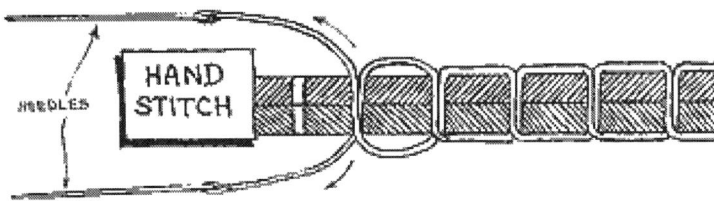

Begin the saddle stitch by pushing a needle through both sides of the aligned holes at one end of a seam. Pull the thread through until equal lengths of thread are on both sides of the leather. Start one needle through the next hole from the same side of the leather. On the other end of the thread, thread a needle and push it through the same hole from the opposite side. Pull both needles through until the stitch is taut. Put equal tension on both needles. Repeat the procedure at the next stitch hole and so on until the end of the seam. Cut off the excess leaving approximately one half to three quarter of an inch past the seam.

Native Reenacting Made Easy

Siege of Boonesborough, 2007 By Graphic Enterprises

Benefits of Wool

Maintains shape when stretched
Remains colorfast when dyed
Wrinkle resistant
Static-free
Soft, durable, and easy to work with
Flame retardant
Water resistant
Wonderful insulator
Breathable
Regulates temperature well

Michael L. Pitzer

Breechclout Overview

Every eastern woodland man used some type of garment to cover the loin area. This was called the breechclout, breechcloth or loincloth. Throughout the ages the function of this garment did not change. Once trade cloth was introduced, the buckskin version of the breechclout was all but replaced. Like the legging, it could be made from several different materials however wool, linen and other trade cloths were most common. I have found linen to be the most comfortable in warm weather. Wool tends to itch a little unless it is lined with another material however it is unsurpassed for its ability to insulate on cold days. In the summer months eastern woodland men would strip down to only a breechclout in order to stay more comfortable. However, traveling warriors would frequently still wear leggings to protect them while traversing heavy underbrush or meadows during hot weather.

In its simplest form, the breechclout was merely a strip of material approximately 12 inches wide by 60 inches long draped between the legs over a thong. The properly fitted Eastern style breechclout should hang approximately 2" to 3" past the crotch in both the front and back. Use a silk scarf or leather thong to tie around the waist. Do not over decorate the breechclout for battle reenactments. Generally, Woodland warriors used silver brooches as trade currency or a symbol of wealth and standing in the tribe.

Silver brooches were generally not worn during an actual battle, but were cached close by so if they were to be killed in battle the others would take fallen warrior's silver to his family.

Note: Do not confuse the eastern and western style of wear. Eastern tribes kept the breechclout short to avoid getting caught on underbrush, whereas the plains tribes would often have breechclouts down past the knees.

Breechclout Materials List

- 2.5 Yards of good quality wool. Preferably black, red or dark blue.
- Spool of heavy linen thread. Choose a color close to the wool color.
- Pair of scissors, a plastic tape measure, needles and beeswax.
- 18 Linear Feet of silk ribbon.
- 1/2 Yard of cotton cloth for the groin pad (optional).

Michael L. Pitzer

Breechclout Construction Details

Step One - Cut a strip of wool that is approximately 60 inches long by 12 inches wide. Find the lengthwise center and measure out about 9 inches in both directions from this point.

Step Two -Mark about 3 inches in on each side. See pattern below. Cutout the 3" by 18" area in the crotch.

Step Three -Make a cloth cutout that matches the crotch area of the garment. This will become your liner.

Step Four - Hand sew the liner into the breechclout taking care to sew all edges (see pattern – dotted lines).

Step Five -Try on the garment and cut the front and rear apron area so that it hangs approximately 3-4 inches below the crotch (Mid Thigh).Once the breechclout fits properly it can be decorated by sewing the silk ribbon material along the edges as piping.

NOTE: You may also want to sew white seed beads along the edge and add silver brooches as a final customization touch.

Native Reenacting Made Easy

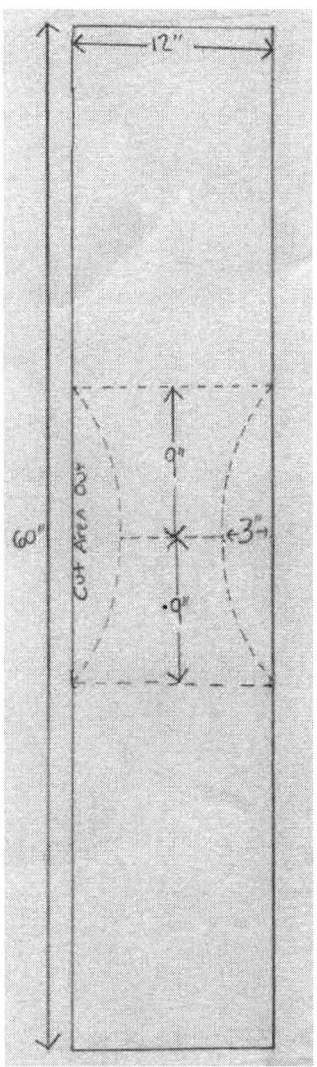

Breechclout Pattern Illustration By Dakota S. Pitzer

Michael L. Pitzer

"How smooth must be the language of the whites, when they can make right look like wrong, and wrong like right."

Black Hawk, Sauk

Chapter Four
Moccasins (M'ki-thai-nah)

Moccasin Overview

After trying several different methods of moccasin construction, I am convinced that Mark Baker's process is the best way to make a serviceable and durable pair of moccasins with the least headaches. Native footwear always varied from tribe to tribe, but all wore some type of shoe sewn from animal hide. The word "moccasin" is derived from an Algonquian word that was utilized nearly universally by whites to describe North American aboriginal footwear. Algonquin tribes were the first Indians encountered by Europeans in the new world and the name stuck as whites migrated westward. This is the reason why all native shoes are called moccasins to this day.

Eastern tribes preferred a one piece moccasin without an added sole because it was easily constructed and very comfortable for walking in heavily wooded areas where leaves cushioned the person's step. Patterns varied somewhat from tribe to tribe. However, observant natives could often tell various tribal affiliations simply from looking at the footwear (Redish & Lewis 1998 – 2008).

Michael L. Pitzer

A major faux pas of the reenactment world is to wear inappropriate footwear to a period event. I will illustrate the differences in authentic versus inappropriate footwear in the next couple of pictures. The moccasin captioned as inappropriate footwear is a finely crafted modernized version (sole added) of the center seam moccasin that would fool the casual observer. However, it has no place at a serious period event. Save them for camping with the family and hunting. The authentic moccasin was constructed with the method described in this text and would be correct for any period event.

Authentic Style of Center Seam Moccasin

Native Reenacting Made Easy

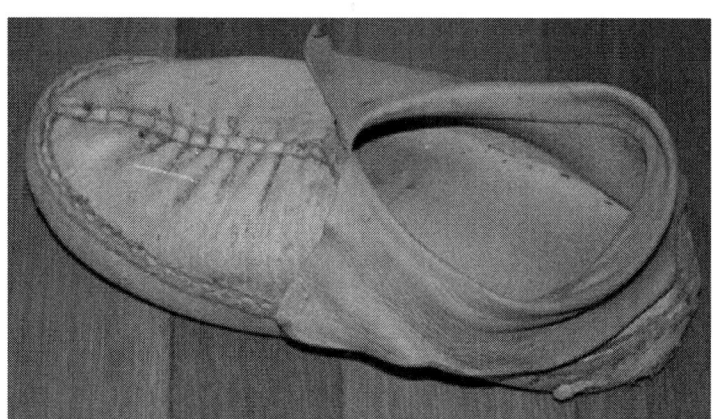

Inappropriate Footwear – Note the seam around the sole

Mark Baker's Moccasin Making Method

This chapter is adapted from a segment of a video series produced by Jim Wright of American Pioneer Video called The Longhunter Series. To create your moccasins, you will begin by finding brain-tan leather from moose, elk, buffalo or some other thick skinned animal. Once you have located suitable leather, find the thickest part of the hide and this should be used for the sole area of the moccasins.

American Pioneer Video can be found on the web at www.americanpioneervideo.com

Michael L. Pitzer

Moccasin Materials List

- Half hide of brain tanned leather such as moose, elk, mule deer or buffalo
- Spool Heavy Linen Thread 4 Ply Recommended
- Pencil, Awl, Plastic Tape Measure, Needles & Beeswax
- Good scissors made for leather crafting.

Game animals are a good source of project leather

Native Reenacting Made Easy

Tips for Getting Hides on the Cheap

Make friends with a serious hunter and ask for the hide of their kills and tan them yourself or offer to provide multiple green hides in exchange for tanned hides from a tanner. Go to game processing stations and ask for hides. They can also provide brains for native style hide tanning.

Moccasin Construction Details

Step One - Begin by folding the leather in half at the thickest part. Set your foot on the leather with the fold to the inside of the leg and trace around your foot taking care to curve out a little at your second toe. Leave about 1/4" around the toes. Stop at the small toe.

Step Two - Using the plastic tape, measure the circumference of your instep approximately 1½" from the base of your leg.

Step Three - Take half of this measurement and place the tape under your foot at the point you measured and mark this point on the leather.

Step Four - Join the point you just marked with the mark where you ended at the small toe and extend it approximately 2" past the heel.

Step Five - Cut out the moccasin taking great care to keep the cuts perpendicular to the floor.

Step Six - Cut out a ¼" welt strip from the main piece of leather (where you cut out the toe of the moccasin).

Step Seven - Cut a piece of 4 ply linen thread 2 1/2 times as long as the instep mark to the big toe and run it through the beeswax several times.

Step Eight - Cut a 45 degree slant on the end of the welt strip and insert it point down (the point will be on the outside once the moccasin is right side out).

Step Nine - Starting at the big toe area, punch a few holes and begin sewing the moccasin together with the welt between the moccasin body. Only punch and sew a few holes at a time to avoid alignment errors later. Use a running stitch.

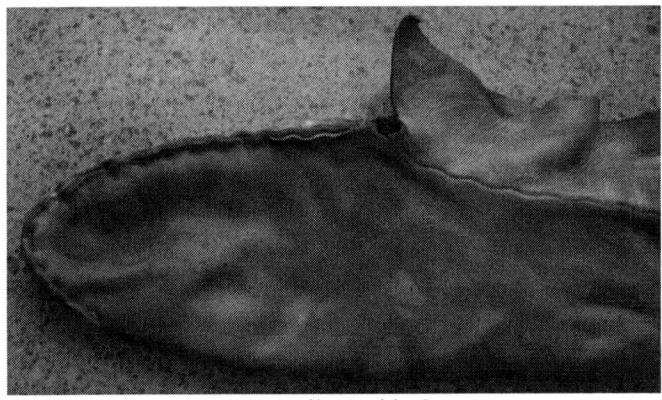

Toe Detail – Inside Out

Native Reenacting Made Easy

Step Ten - Stop at your instep mark and make several loops on the instep stop point to increase durability.

Step Eleven - Turn the sewn are inside out and trim the excess welt. If threads are visible take it apart and re-sew it. Otherwise it will not hold up to real use.

Step Twelve - Try it on. The seam should run up the top of the foot. Pull it over your toes tightly and mark your heel on the inside (sole area).

Step Thirteen - Pinch the leather together down the back and mark the line down to the heel from your ankle (line along the back of the leg).

Step Fourteen - Flatten out the moccasin on its side and find your heel to ankle marks. Make a mark approximately 1" past the back of the leg to heel line and cut off the excess.

Step Fifteen - Turn it inside out again (same as when you sewed the toes) and sew in a 1/4" welt stopping about one inch before reaching the heel along the line marked down the back of the leg.

Step Sixteen - With the toe seam perpendicular to the ground push the heel until the unsewn portion flattens out to the ground. It should an inverted "T" shape about as wide as your heel. On the two edges touching the ground make two cuts to the back of the heel.

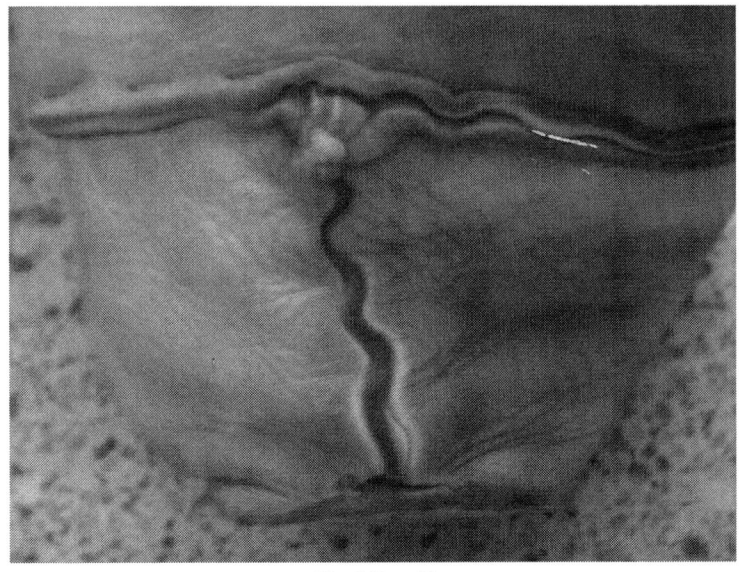

Heel Detail

Step Seventeen - Tuck the "flap inside and then sew along the two incisions you just made.

Step Eighteen - Turn it inside out again and try it on. The moccasin should fit snugly at this point (leather will stretch with use).

Step Nineteen - Measure the open top area around the ankle and add 3" to that measurement.

Step Twenty - Transfer that measurement to the main piece of leather and mark it. Cut out two flaps that are the length you just marked and about 3 ½" wide.

Step Twenty One- Cut out the flaps.

Step Twenty Two- Tuck the flaps into the moccasin and sew them using a running stitch. Flip them to the outside and the seam should be hidden.

Cuff Detail

Step Twenty Three- Add a lace strap around the ankle and repeat for moccasin number two.

Michael L. Pitzer

NOTE: If you are not a hard core traditionalist, comfort may be added to your moccasins by inserting a modern insole inside. Only your 21st century feet will know you are gellin.

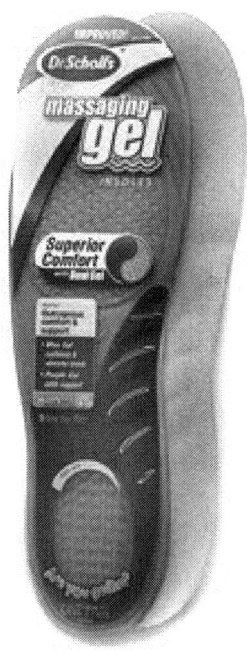

Dr. Scholls® Massaging Gel Insert

Native Reenacting Made Easy

Battle of Blue Licks, 2008 by Graphic Enterprises

Battle of Blue Licks, 2006 by Graphic Enterprises

Michael L. Pitzer

"When your time comes to die, be not like those whose hearts are filled with fear of death, so that when their time comes they weep and pray for a little more time to live their lives over again in a different way. Sing your death song, and die like a hero going home"

Tecumseh, Shawnee

Chapter Five
Trade Shirts (Peleneca)

Trade Shirt Overview

The trade shirt was one of the most coveted items on an Indian's trade list. The shirt was one of the first items to be stripped from the body of a fallen soldier after a battle due to the utilitarian value of it. As a reenactor you have two choices with regard to trade shirts; buy one or make it from scratch. Given the effort involved in making one, I would strongly recommend buying it from one of the many sutlers at the period trade fairs (I buy from Timberline Traders - See Resources). However, If you are committed to the idea of making your own shirt, I would highly recommend, supplementing this chapter with "Tidings from the 18th Century" - by Beth Gilgun. ISBN: 1880655047; Scurlock Publishing Co. (903-832-4726) This book has an excellent pattern for a simple shirt and will guide you through all the intricate details involved.

What Color & Type of Cloth?

There are several choices available; however research suggests that a plain off-white linen or a navy/white checked pattern would be most appropriate.

Michael L. Pitzer

Neck and/or wrist ruffles are an option if you wish to portray a chief or high status native. Cotton was available near the end of the Revolutionary War period, but was less common than linen. Calico prints were also traded to native people during the 18th century but were also were less abundant on the frontier than just plain linen shirts. That being said, I would not recommend using either for your shirt unless you have good reasons for doing so.

If you plan to spend a lot of time in the woods and would like to tone down the look of a stark white shirt, soak the fabric in tea or use a natural colored linen material rather than bright white to make the shirt. You can also use walnut hull dye to tone it down but don't over do it. Your shirt should be mid-thigh in length so it can protect your legs from underbrush. In addition to dying the fabric, you may want to consider making your shirt look very dirty by distressing it with wood ash, dirt, etc. This adds to your impression and creates a "believable" image.

NOTE: Please understand that this is an oversimplified how-to overview of a very complex project. I do not claim to be a tailor, therefore, I highly recommend that you find a detailed pattern for this project before beginning. Hand sewing all visible seams is recommended for the sake of realism. All seams should have 12 stitches per inch.

Native Reenacting Made Easy

Example of a distressed shirt

Trade Shirt Materials List

- 3 Yards of 42" Wide material such as Linen in a subdued natural color.
- Spool of Linen Thread.
- Pencil, Scissors, Awl, Plastic Tape Measure, Needles, Pins.
- Detailed Pattern Book such as Tidings from the 18th Century"- by Beth Gilgun

Shirt Cut List

Body -30" X 80"* -Rectangular -1

Sleeves -20" X 20"* -Rectangular -2

Arm Pit Gusset -6" X 6" -Square -2

Cuffs -5" X 13"* -Rectangular -2

Collar -10" X 19"* -Rectangular -1

Neck Gusset -4" X 4" -Square -2

Shoulder Strips -2" X 4" -Rectangular -(2) opt

Front Gusset -3" X 3" -Square -(2) opt

* Use Your Measurements - Rough Estimate

Trade Shirt Construction Details

Step One - Take the plastic tape measure and drape it over your shoulder and use it to determine the overall length needed to create the body of the garment. Remember to make it long enough to hit at least mid-thigh.

Step Two - Now measure the width of your shoulders and transfer the measurements onto your fabric.

Step Three - Cut out the body of the garment and fold it in half so that it could be placed over your head if a neck hole was cut.

Step Four - At the fold, find the center point across the width of the fabric. Mark 8" inches on each side of this center point (head hole).

Step Five - From the center point, mark a 10" line down the center on the front of the body.

Step Six - Cut along the 16" Mark.

Step Seven - Cut along the 10" mark and fold back about ¼" of material to the inside and hand stitch it into place creating a "V" in the neck.

Step Eight - Sew in the "Front Seam Gusset" at the bottom of the "V" in the neck to reinforce the bottom of the opening.

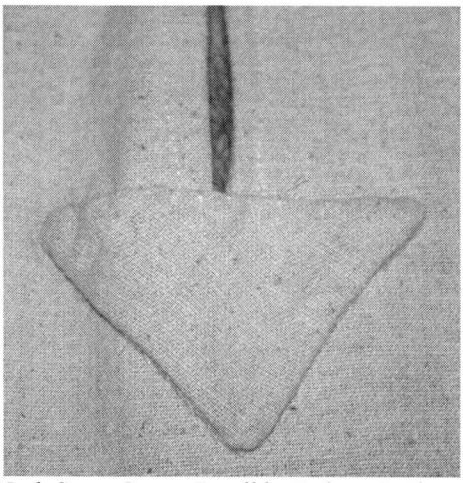

Neck Seam Gusset Detail by Dakota S. Pitzer

Step Nine - Sew in "Neck Gussets" at the ends of the neck opening to reinforce the area of the opening nearest the shoulders.

Step Ten - Fold the "Collar" in half lengthwise and sew in around the neck opening.

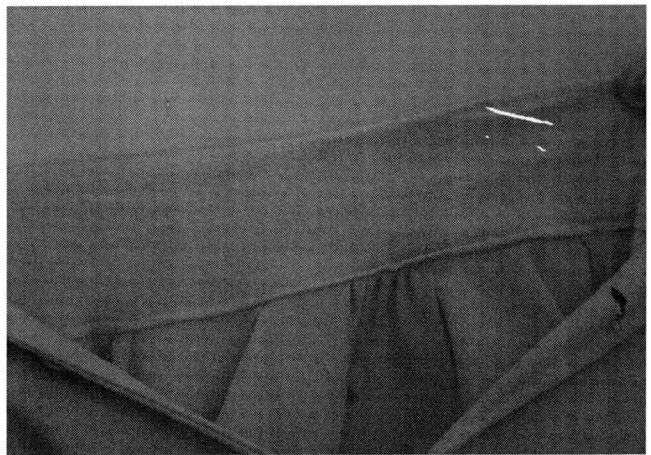

Collar Detail by Dakota S. Pitzer

Step Eleven - Sew in the "Shoulder Patches". They should be sewn inside the shoulder area parallel to the sleeve openings (front to back of body).

Step Twelve - Sew the sleeves together and place the "Arm Pit Gusset" in one end of the sleeve (placement of the gusset should be in the form of a diamond to the sleeve).

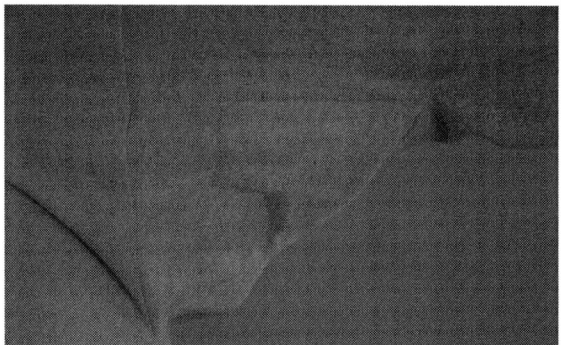

Arm Pit Gusset Detail by Dakota S. Pitzer

Step Thirteen - Sew the sleeves to the body and then attach the cuffs to the sleeves.

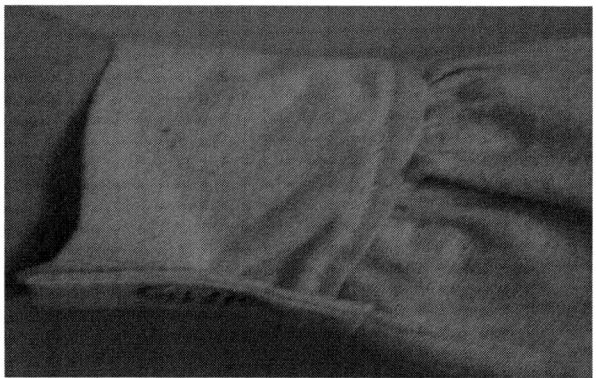

Cuff Detail by Dakota S. Pitzer

Step Fourteen - Make two slits at the bottom of the shirt (side area) and fold back ¼" like you did in the neck area to stop unraveling.

Step Fifteen - Attach buttons, distress and wear.

Michael L. Pitzer

Making Fabric Block Printing Ink

Research suggests that block printed fabrics were fairly popular in the late 18th century. Before taking on a project such as this, I would recommend researching common patterns through primary sources.

Homemade Ink Materials List

- Five Tablespoons of Turpentine
- Two Tablespoons of Vinegar
- Tablespoon of Wintergreen Oil
- Tablespoon of Liquid Dish Washing Soap
- Eight Ounce Bottle
- Multiple Oil Paint Pigments
- Palette Knife
- Sheet of Glass
- Brayer aka craft roller
- Carved wood or linoleum block (pattern)
- Fabric
- Hot Iron

Native Reenacting Made Easy

Ink Making Process Details

Step One - Pour the first 4 ingredients into a bottle and shake well.

Step Two - Add oil paint pigments until you get a thick creamy consistency and the desired color.

Instructions For Using the Ink

Step One - Smooth with a palette knife on a sheet of glass.

Step Two - Roll brayer back and forth until mixture is tacky and the brayer is evenly coated.

Step Three - Roll the brayer over the carved block.

Step Four - Press the block onto fabric and press evenly with all your weight.

Step Five - Lift the block from the fabric and place a damp cloth over the design.

Step Six - Press the cloth with a hot iron.

Step Seven - The patterned fabric can be washed in warm water with a mild soap (CanTeach, 1998).

Michael L. Pitzer

"Englishmen, although you have conquered the French, you have not yet conquered us. We are not your slaves. These lakes, these woods and mountains were left us by our ancestors. We will part with them to no one."

Pontiac, Ottawa

Chapter Six
Bags (Posan) & Accessories

Native Style Shoulder Bag

Native American bags came in many shapes and sizes and they were generally of the open top variety. They may or may not have included a false flap front, deer tassels, seed beads and quill work. Without exception, they were worn high on the ribcage and tight to the body in order to allow quiet movement through the woods.

The rough dimension of this type of bag is approximately 10" wide by 8" tall. You can make it out of any color of leather you wish but darker colors look more authentic. Adjust the dimensions to suit your individual taste and needs. The strap can be made from leather, braided twine, woven fabric of a combination of materials. Decorative quill and seed bead work was common on the shoulder strap as well as the bag itself. Refrain from hanging gear on the bag strap, warriors preferred not to do this because of noise and entanglement problems when stalking through the woods.

Michael L. Pitzer

Native Bag Materials List

- 10" X 16" of brain tanned leather.
- Spool of heavy linen thread (4 ply recommended) in a color close to the leather color.
- Needles, scissors, awl, pencil, beeswax and a plastic tape measure.
- Good scissors made for leather crafting.
- Several seed beads – white.
- Tanned deer tail.
- Rit brand scarlet dye.
- Brass cones - make or buy

Making Dyed Hair Cone Tassels

Step One - Starting with a tanned deer tail, snip several small squares of hide off with hair still attached.

Step Two - Put them into Rit® Brand Scarlet Dye.

Step Three - Attach a string to the part where hide and hair meet and pull into a brass cone with a drop of glue inside.

Native Reenacting Made Easy

Shoulder Bag Construction Details

Step One - Cut a rectangle that is approximately 10" wide by 16" long. This will be the body of the bag.

Step Two - Place the leather into a walnut hull dye for nearly one week.

Step Three - Fold the leather in half on the 16" side. You should now have a bag that is 10" wide by 8" tall. The folded area will be the bottom of the bag.

Step Four - Sew the sides using a saddle stitch.

Step Five - Add a strap and decorate to taste.

NOTE: Common decorations included sewing a silk ribbon along the top opening, adding a false flap, adding dyed deer tail cone tassels, quill work and sewing on white seed beads.

Michael L. Pitzer

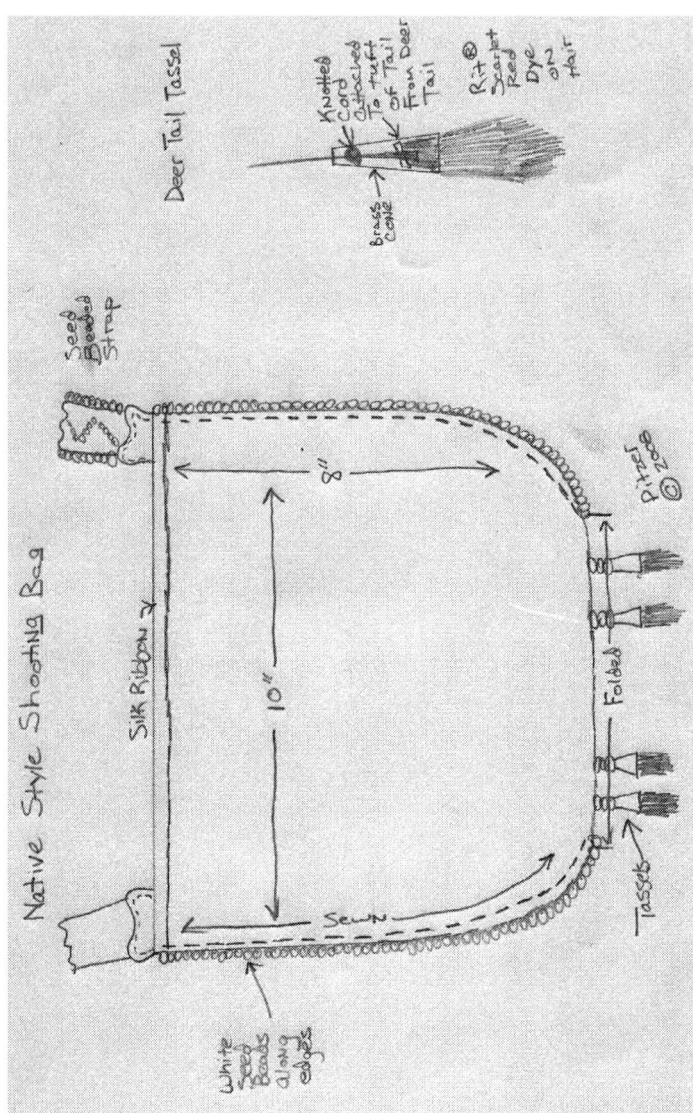

Native Style Bag Sketch

Native Reenacting Made Easy

Garters or Leg Ties

Garters or leg ties are in the simplest form a strip of leather tied over the legging below the knees. The purpose of the garter is to help keep the leggings in place. Garters can be as fancy or as plain as one wants. They can range from leather ties to wampum beads that have been loomed and attached to a hide backing. Other options are to buy garters made by other enthusiasts, create a set of woven garters on a finger loom or to make your own wampum beaded pattern and sew it on a thin leather backing.

Garter Materials List

- Two Pieces of thin and pliable brain tanned leather - measurement of leg below knee plus 5" for each.
- Two Pieces wool – red, blue, black or white preferred.
- Spool heavy linen thread - 4 ply recommended.
- Needles, scissors, awl, pencil, beeswax and a plastic tape measure.
- Good scissors made for leather.
- Several seed beads in a contrasting color.
- Deer hair tassels set in brass cones.

Michael L. Pitzer

Garter Construction Details

Step One - Cut a leather rectangle that is approximately two and one half inches (2.5") wide by the length of your measurement around the leg just below the knee plus five inches (5") long. This will be the backing of the garter and the ties.

Step Two - Cut a wool rectangle that is approximately two and one half inches (2.5") wide by the length of your measurement around the leg just below the knee minus six inches (6") long. This will be the front of the garter.

Step Three - Sew the wool onto the leather.

Step Four - Cut the ties as shown in the diagram.

Step Five - Decorate the garter by sewing on seed beads along the top and bottom edges.

Step Six - Add two deer hair tassels.

NOTE: Ties may be sewn on as shown on the diagram or made as part of the garter.

Native Reenacting Made Easy

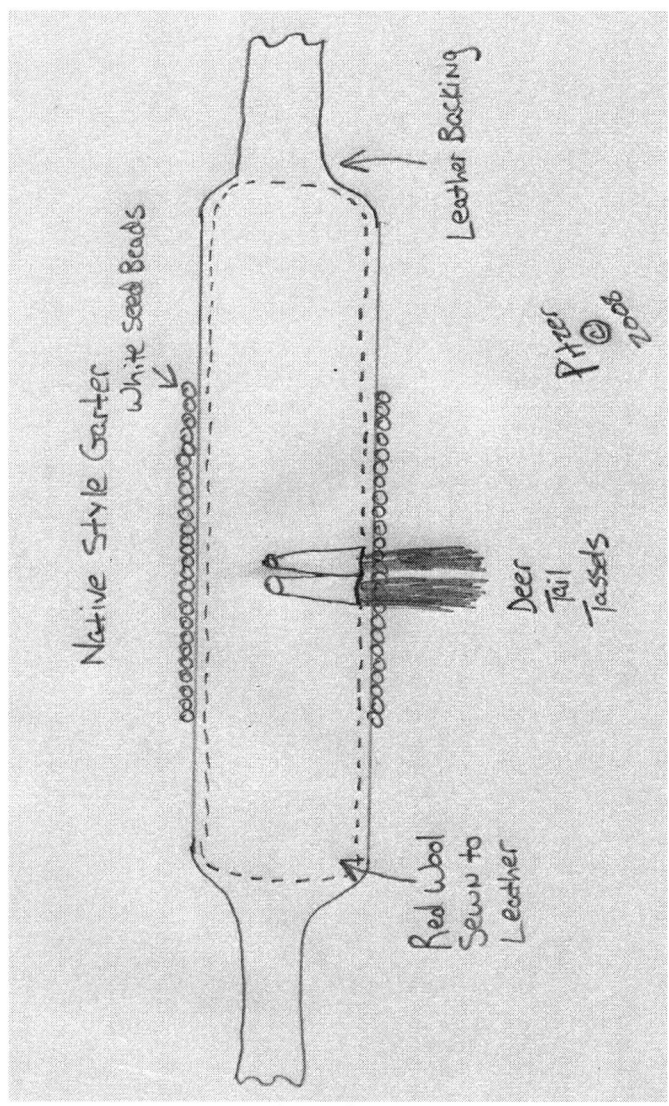

Native Style Garter

Michael L. Pitzer

Finger Woven Wool Sash

Your kit is not complete without a wool finger woven chevron pattern or plain sash. This item should be tied in the back and will be used to tuck miscellaneous items into such as your war club, tomahawk or belt knife. I recommend that you purchase this item due to the skill and time required to make it. I have found them at trade fairs for as little as $30.00 and as much as $200.00. Make sure you research colors worn by the tribe you wish to portray before buying.

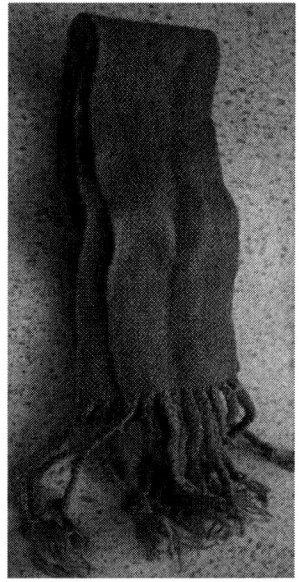

Wool Sash purchased at the Fort Boonesborough Transylvania Store for $25.00 in 2008

Native Reenacting Made Easy

Basic Native Equipment List

Cooking Gear

- Strike-A-Light Kit - flint, steel, tinder.
- Period Correct Cooking Pot- tin or brass.
- Personal eating utensils - wooden noggin and a horn, wood or silver spoon.
- Knife – food preparation, belt or neck knife.
- Water gourd with a rawhide strap – Many groups require that it be carried during battles as well

Sleeping Gear

- Woolen blanket & Period Blanket Pins – To form a crude sleeping bag.
- Tumpline - Leather straps with leather ties appear in period documentation.
- Small leather bags - for storing your small items when not rolled up in your bedroll.
- Optional Groundcloth/shelter - 8' X 8' oilskin tarp.

Michael L. Pitzer

Personal items

- Nick-Knacks - Pipes, tobacco, combs, small trade items, etc. appear regularly in accounts and lists from the period.
- Sewing kit: needles, thread, period correct scissors, leather, various mending materials.
- Mirror, comb, paint kit.
- Period gaming pieces such as gambling sticks can help to pass the time

Accoutrements

- Native Style Shoulder Bag.
- Paper powder charges – for battles.
- Captive rope – used to lead captives from the field.
- Weapons – see chapters on this

Modern Items

- Medications.
- Shaving kits.
- Personal hygiene items, etc.

These items (other than prescriptions) should be stored in period containers and hidden from view of spectators. Try to stay in character as much as possible when in public or displaying gear. Remember, it is illegal to remove prescription medication from its original container. Put the entire medicine bottle(s) into a leather bag.

This checklist adapted from Southern Indian Department's website.

Michael L. Pitzer

"My son, you are now flesh of our flesh and bone of our bone. By the ceremony performed this day, every drop of white blood was washed from your veins; you were taken into the Shawnee Nation...you were adopted into a great family."

Black Fish, Shawnee, 1778

Chapter Seven
Paint & Scalplocks

Paint Overview

Most people's individual characteristics are considered to be their facial features, hair, etc. From birth, human beings are conditioned to recognize family, friends and foes from these features. Don't believe me? Think about a friend or loved one, what was the first thing that popped into your mind? I'll bet it was their face. Native warriors figured out that by obscuring their natural individual characteristics such as the face it can send chills down the spine of an enemy facing them in battle. For centuries, native warriors used this fear to their advantage by looking so frightening that the enemy would rather flee than fight.

Good body painting can make or break your impression. Few things will ruin a reenactor's appearance faster than face painting that looks like a Tammy Faye Baker makeover. Painting on inappropriate colors and patterns not only looks horrible but is also is very disrespectful to the culture you are trying to represent. (Mott & Obermeyer, 1990).

Michael L. Pitzer

The Meaning of Each Color

Colors and symbols used in battle had significant meaning to the wearer. Unfortunately, very little factual historical information has survived as to what colors and patterns were really used and why. Color meanings varied from tribe to tribe so these color definitions are just generally accepted interpretations.

RED (Mesquaway) – Worn when seeking vengeance or retribution. Symbolically it represents the blood that a warrior intended to spill. It was the color of war. (Mott & Obermeyer, 1990).

BLACK (Cuttaywah) – Was applied to cut-a-hotha (condemned men) when being led to their death through Shawnee, Mingo, Delaware & Wyandott villages. The condemned prisoner was completely covered in black (Eckert 2001). Other tribes considered it the color of life and it was worn on the face to let the enemy know you may take captives or show mercy. It was revered for the terrifying presence it created (Mott & Obermeyer, 1990).

WHITE (Wahcanaquah) - Color of peace Indians knew that the white man respected this color as a sign of peace. (Mott & Obermeyer, 1990).

GREEN (Skeporscotto) – Under the eyes makes for better night sight or extra-ordinary night vision powers. (Mott & Obermeyer, 1990).

YELLOW (Hoθaawa) – Signifies death because it resembles "aged bone". It also signifies a man has lived his life and will fight to the finish (Mott & Obermeyer, 1990).

Paint Safety 101

Non-Toxic does not mean safe for your body. Acrylic craft paints are not safe for the skin. Many people have strong allergic reactions to some of the chemicals and colorants used in craft paints (such as nickel). Reactions can be as minor as a rash and as severe as death (Trusty, Date Unknown). In addition to being unsafe to use on skin, the aforementioned paints are not authentic. Chances are that you will look more like a rodeo clown than a woodland warrior if you wear some of these paints. 18th century natives made their paints from plants, berries, charcoal and minerals. If you are inclined to make your own paints, it can be done with relative ease. However, I just buy mine from Crazy Crow Trading Post (www.crazycrow.com). Their powders are good and will not adversely impact your budget. In addition, their powdered paint is all natural and safe for use on even the most sensitive skin. A jar the size shown below costs around $2.95 and several authentic colors are available.

Michael L. Pitzer

Creating a Paint Kit

All serious reenactors should create a paint kit. While it seems self explanatory, here are some tips that will save you aggravation and money. Begin by finding or making a deer skin pouch or other suitable carrying case. This will go to every reenactment you attend, so put some thought into it. You will also need some small tins with secure lids or plugged cane containers to store your powdered paints in.

Battle of Blue Licks, 2006 by Graphic Enterprises

Native Reenacting Made Easy

Paint Kit Materials List

- Jar of Red, Black, Yellow, Green & White Powdered Paint from Crazy Crow Trading Post $2.95 Jar. Small amount of olive oil, deer or bear tallow if a purist.
- Three freshwater mussel shells or other small dishes - can be wood, metal, shell, stone, etc.
- Period correct mirror - crude & homemade preferred.
- Jar of cold cream - Pond's or generic.
- Five small tins that close securely for powdered paints.
- Two small period type bottles for oil, tallow, and cold cream.
- Leather bag for holding everything.
- Sock filled with red iron oxide, aka Texas dust bag.

Michael L. Pitzer

How to Use Your Paint Kit

Step One - Shave all body hair that will be painted and wash all exposed skin thoroughly.

Step Two - Apply the cold cream to your bare skin and allow it to dry.

Step Three - Pull out your mussel shells and put a little powdered paint into them (one color per shell).

Step Four - Pour a little oil/tallow into the shell and mix until paint is consistent in texture and color.

Step Five - Paint as desired and apply the Texas dust on any uncovered exposed skin.

TIP: If you need to scratch while in paint, use a small stick and poke it at the offending spot. This also works for sweat beads in hot weather.

You may also choose to get a spray tan from one of the commercial tanning operations near you. This may be a good approach for a multiple day event where showering is not possible.

Paint Kit Details

Place the powdered paints into the small tins. One color per tin. Birch or cane containers may be substituted for the tins. Put the oil into some type of water tight spill free container. Store the cold cream in a similar way.

1830s lithograph based on the last portrait of Brant, an 1806 oil on canvas painting by Ezra Ames

Michael L. Pitzer

Examples of Face Paint

Battle of Blue Licks, 2006 by Graphic Enterprises

Siege of Boonesborough, 2007 by Graphic Enterprises

Prosthetic Scalp Locks

Throughout history, warrior cultures have thought that certain parts of the body contain mystical powers. The American Indian was no different. They believed that the scalp was connected to their fate, therefore a warrior's scalp lock represented his life to him. (Drimmer, 1985).

In Daniel Boone's captivity among the Shawnee, the scalp-lock is described as follows: "The ceremony of adoption was pretty severe and painful. All the hair of the head was plucked out by a tedious operation, leaving simply a tuft three or four inches in diameter on the crown. This was called the scalp lock. The hair was here allowed to grow long, and was dressed with ribbons and feathers. It was to an individual warrior what the banner is to an army. The victor tore it from the skull as his trophy. Having thus denuded the head and dressed the scalp-lock, the candidate was taken to the river and very thoroughly scrubbed, that all the white blood might be washed out of him"(Abbott, 1874, Pages 198 -199).

In the mentality of the Eastern Woodland warrior a scalp lock was a dare to the enemy to "come and take it" if he could. Typically, the scalp lock would be divided in three parts. The first was a long braid extending down to the neck and the other two were wrapped with quills forcing them to stand prominently above the head (Hartman, Hudson, Lee & Heath, 2000).

Michael L. Pitzer

Scalp Lock Materials List

- Crown weave preferably black human hair.
- Tube of spirit gum
- Three leather ties

Scalp Lock Construction & Use Details

Step One - Trim the crown weave to size (about 4" diameter circle) and Braid the hair into 3 separate tufts. One about 8" long and two 4" long braids.

Step Two - Tie off the ends of each braid with the leather ties.

Step Three - Smear spirit gum to the underside of the scalp lock and clean your head with alcohol where you intend to attach the lock.

Step Four - Smear the attaching spot on your head with spirit gum and allow it to tack for about 5 minutes. Attach the scalp lock.

Step Five - Decorate with a porky, hackle feather or a turkey roach.

Native Reenacting Made Easy

Long Run Massacre, 2008 by Graphic Enterprises

Siege of Boonesborough, 2007 by Graphic Enterprises

Michael L. Pitzer

"The Whites are already nearly a match for us all united, and too strong for any one tribe alone to resist. Unless we support one another with our collective forces, they will soon conquer us, and we will be driven away from our native country and scattered as leaves before the wind."

Tecumseh, Shawnee

Chapter Eight
Weapons

Rifle Versus Smooth Bore

While Eastern tribes undoubtedly traded for and used rifles during the 18th century, smooth bores were more common and more versatile to native warriors. In addition, at living history events, rifles tend to clog up faster when doing battle scenes and don't make as much noise as smooth bores. These two reasons alone should be enough to make you want one.

When choosing an appropriate weapon (gun) for living history events, your tribal affiliation and era of interest will dictate which gun is correct for your persona. If in doubt, you can always carry a gun that is older than your era but you can't carry something newer. Native reenactors will probably want to stick with a plain military grade French Tulle de Chasse, Brown Bess or Trade gun. You should strive to be as ordinary as possible in your interpretation. Entire books are devoted to the topic of firearms; therefore I do not plan to go into much depth here.

Michael L. Pitzer

Charleville Musket

The Charleville musket was a .69 caliber French musket used in the 18th and 19th centuries. It was named after the armory in Charleville-Mézières, Ardennes, France. A standardized version of the musket was first created in 1717. The 1717 was replaced eleven years later in 1728 with a model using three barrel bands to hold its 46 3/4 inch barrel in place. Changes in the 1740s included the standardized use of a steel ramrod in 1743 and, after 1746, newly manufactured muskets had the pan/frizzen bridle removed. Further refinements were made in the 1750's and 1760's. In 1763 a new model was produced which was stronger than the previous version. The Model 1763 proved to be too heavy, and was replaced by a lighter version in 1766. Minor refinements continued until 1777.

The Charleville musket had a .69 caliber barrel, which was smaller than the .75 caliber Brown Bess produced by the British. The rate of fire depended on the skill of the soldier, which was typically about 2-3 shots per minute. Smooth bore muskets in general have an accuracy of only about 50 to 100 meters, and hitting anything beyond 200 meters is mostly a matter of luck. Because of this, combat tended to be at fairly close range, and bayonet fighting often determined the outcome of battles. In general, bayonets accounted for 30 to 40 percent of casualties during battles with smooth bore muskets like the Charleville. The Charleville musket was used by the Canadian Militia from the early 1700s to the early 1800s. It was also used by the French during their participation in the American Revolutionary War and throughout the French Revolutionary and Napoleonic Wars. Large numbers of Charleville muskets were imported into the United States from France during the American Revolution, due in large part to the influence of Marquis de Lafayette. The Charleville musket heavily influenced the design of the Springfield Musket of 1795 (Wikipedia, 2009).

Brown Bess

Brown Bess is a nickname of uncertain origin for the British Army's Land Pattern Musket and its derivatives. This musket was in use for over a hundred years with many incremental changes in its design. These versions include the Long Land Pattern, Short Land Pattern, India Pattern, New Land Pattern Musket, Sea Service Musket and others. The Long Land Pattern musket and its derivatives, all .75 caliber flintlock muskets, were the standard long guns of the British Empire's land forces from 1722 until 1838.

Michael L. Pitzer

Most male citizens of the American Colonies were required by law to own arms and ammunition for militia duty; the Long Land Pattern was a common firearm in use by both sides at the commencement of the American Revolution (Wikipedia, 2009). This weapon was commonly carried by British Native allies in the French & Indian War as well as the American Revolution. These weapons were also picked up by British enemies on the battlefield as well.

Fusil de Chasse Tulle

Photo: Track of the Wolf

The Tulle was a .62 caliber smooth bore originally made in France, at the Tulle arsenal, or at Saint Etienne, the French trade gun known as the fusil-de-chasse was a light weight gun-for-the-hunt. The stock architecture and iron trim resemble those of the heavier French military muskets, but are lighter, and more slender. This is the choice gun for any serious native interpreter from the French & Indian War all the way through the War of 1812. (Track of the Wolf, 2009).

I personally find the Tulle to be a well balanced and fun weapon to shoot. The smooth bore allows for easy loading and you can shoot both shot and ball when hunting with it.

Trade Guns

Fur Trade Companies were importing Trade Guns before 1690, and they were popular in the Northern United States and Canada, until 1890. Powerful, inexpensive, and cheap to shoot, Trade Guns were made before the Brown Bess was standardized. Made primarily for the Canadian fur trade, Northwest Guns were found around the world. One well made specimen was marked by the Committee of Safety, for defense during the American Revolution. (Track of the Wolf, 2009).

Making reenactment Powder Charges

Powder Charge Materials List

- Sheet of paper such as a period newspaper reprint.
- 90 Grains of black powder for .62 Caliber.
- Magic marker.
- Pair of scissors
- 12" Jute twine

Michael L. Pitzer

Powder Charge Construction Details

Step One - Trim the newspaper into a rectangle approximately six inches (6") long by four inches (4") wide.

Step Two - Use the magic marker to roll up a tube that is six inches (6") long.

Step Three - Twist one end of the tube and tie it with the twine.

Step Four - Remove the marker and fill the tube with your pre-measured charge of powder, twist the end closed and tie it with the twine.

Using Your Powder Charges

Step One - Tear off one end of the "cartridge".

Step Two - Pour most of the powder down your barrel (keep your face back).

Step Three - Use the remainder to prime.

Step Four - Place the paper trash into your shoulder bag.

Step Five - Fire when ready.

War Clubs

There were several types of war clubs in use throughout the Great Lakes region long before the 18th century. However, the most common surviving examples seem to be the ball-headed style war club. The Eastern club was generally crafted from a root burl of a small hard-wood tree such as an ash or maple. It was the preferred close quarters weapon for native warriors in the Great Lakes region and beyond. The shaft of a club was sometimes engraved with images that bore significance to its owner such as an animal associated with their clan, or their dodem, an Algonquian word for a warrior's guardian spirit. Additionally, incised lines were sometimes added to represent a record of the owner's exploits in battle. (McCord Museum of Canadian History, Date Unknown).

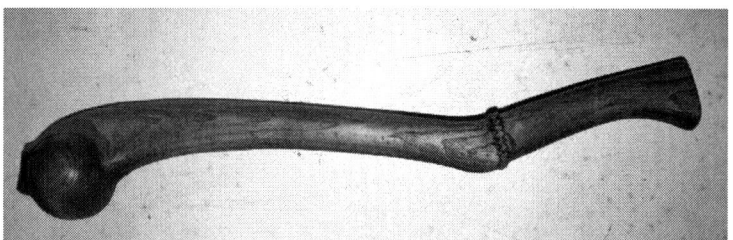

Mingo (Seneca) Style – Hind Leg Ball Headed Club

Michael L. Pitzer

Belt Axes

Some sanctioning bodies have rules against carrying edged weapons on the battle field during battle reenactments; however that doesn't mean you shouldn't have them around camp. Aside from being something that a native would not be caught without, they are invaluable around the campsite. Most new reenactors rush out and buy a throwing tomahawk; I recommend not doing this unless throwing a hawk in competition is something you are interested in exploring. Natives liked pipe hawks, small polled axes and belt axes because they could serve multiple purposes. Below is a photograph of my favorite belt ax. It was purchased for about $35.00 from R.E. Davis Company.

Mohawk Belt Ax – Copied from an excavated original

Knives

Probably the first investment that you should make as a new reenactor is a quality handmade neck knife and quilled sheath. I drive my wife crazy every time we go to a trade fair because I always seem to find another knife that I can't live without. If you are like me, you just can't have enough knives. This particular roach-belly knife was purchased for $25.00 from Fort Boonesborough's Transylvania Store and the sheath came from Corum Knives ($110.00).

Roach Belly Knife with Quilled Neck Sheath

Corum French Style Knife, Medium Sized

Native Reenacting Made Easy

English Scalping Knife with a handmade sheath from Dixie Gun Works

Michael L. Pitzer

Hay fork Tine Neck Knife with a Rawhide Sheath

This nice little patch knife was purchased from Jay 2-Hawks at the Friendship National Shoot in 2005 for about $45.00 and included the sheath. I haven't seen Jay since purchasing this knife, but he makes a great knife and I would love another one if anyone knows how to contact him.

Choosing what type of knife to carry is a very personal decision that you must make depending on what feels best in your hand. As a general rule, I try to buy multipurpose blades that are useful while hunting, participating in reenactments or working around camp. If you buy a quality blade and sheath, you will never be disappointed.

Native Reenacting Made Easy

Siege of Boonesborough, 2007 by Graphic Enterprises

Michael L. Pitzer

"When a white army battles Indians and wins, it is called a great victory, but if they lose it is called a massacre."

Chiksika, Shawnee

Chapter Nine
Homemade Gunpowder (Macate)

Leaching Your Own Potassium Nitrate

On almost a daily basis, it seems like the government enacts some new law to "protect" us from ourselves. That being said, a day may come when purchasing a pound of black powder will require government permits and other bureaucratic red tape or may not be available at all. In the spirit of the era we like to portray, I will show you how to make your own gunpowder from scratch with commonly available materials. Please do not misunderstand my intentions, I do not advocate breaking the law and at the time of this writing it is not unlawful to make your own gun powder. The true purpose of this chapter is to teach you a skill that will enable you to remain self sufficient in difficult years to come.

Leaching Materials List
- Shovel.
- Two five gallon buckets with Lids.
- Ten gallons of suitable soil from an area where livestock frequently urinate and defecate - Chicken coups, horse stalls and dog "potty areas".
- Two metal buckets - Perforate the bottom of one of the buckets.
- ½ Yard of cloth - Must be porous.
- ½ Gallon of white wood ashes.

- Two gallons of distilled water - Rain water is also OK.
- Heat Source – Outdoors.
- Wooden spoon.
- Mortar and pestle.

Leaching Process Details

Step One - Take a shovel and two five gallon buckets with lids to an area where livestock frequently urinate and defecate (chicken coup, barn, horse stalls, etc). Fill up the buckets with the blackest soil you find and take them back home.

Step Two - Get a metal bucket and punch several holes into the bottom of it. Next lay a heavy piece of cloth over the holes (inside the bucket) and spread approximately a ½ cup of clean white wood ash over the cloth on the bottom of the bucket. Place a second cloth over top of the wood ash and then fill the bucket to about 2" from the top with the soil you dug up.

Step Three - Set this bucket over a slightly smaller metal bucket and pour about 1 ½ gallons of boiling water over the dirt and allow it to drain for a few hours.

Step Four - Separate the two buckets and bring the liquid to a boil and keep it simmering. Tiny grains of salt will begin to form and you need to scoop these out with a wooden spoon and throw them away.

Step Five - Continue simmering until about 1/3 of the liquid remains. Remove from the heat source and allow it to cool for a couple of hours. Potassium Nitrate crystals will begin to form. Strain out these crystals and set them aside to dry. Once they have dried the potassium nitrate is ready to be ground into a fine powder (Hooker 2007 Pages 45-46 Backwoodsman Magazine).

Making Pyrotechnic Grade Charcoal

Charcoal is the big variable when making black powder. Using commercial briquettes is going to make lousy black powder. The reason for this is that most commercial charcoals are made from hardwood with clay, coal, and other materials added to the powdered charcoal for the purpose of pressing the charcoal into the familiar briquette shape. These impurities dilute the carbon content thus causing inferior gun powder. This method adapted from an article that was retrieved August 13, 2008 from www.wichitabuggywhip.com. All photos were taken by the online source.

Michael L. Pitzer

Charcoal Making Materials List

Empty one gallon paint can with lid - New preferred, buy from paint store.
Empty Five Gallon Metal Can - Any will work.
6' Untreated white pine 2X4 - Split into 1/2" x 7" long slivers.
Fire Brick - A landscaping Brick will also work.
Bag commercial charcoal - To be used as a heat source

Charcoal Making Process Details

Step One - Drill about twenty five 1/2" holes in the lower sides of the five gallon can.

Step Two - Drill a 1/2" hole in the lid of the one gallon can.

Example of Step Two

Step Three - Place the fire brick in the bottom of the can and add charcoal until it is level with the brick.

Step Four - Fill the one gallon can with 1/2" wide by 7" slivers of your wood. Don't pack wood too tight. Leave enough air space that it doesn't insulate itself.

Example of Step Four

Step Five - Put the lid on the small can. Light the commercial charcoal in the five gallon can and put the one gallon can on top then fill in the sides with more charcoal.

Step Six - Let it cook until gases stop coming out of the 1/2" hole in the top of the one gallon can (1-3 hours).

Step Seven - Let it cool completely - then open can.

Step Eight - Crush the charcoal until it reaches air float consistency (black dust so fine it lingers in the air when disturbed).

Michael L. Pitzer

Sugar From Sap

Several species of maples grow throughout the United States. All species can be used to make syrup. However, sugar maple (acer saccharum) and black maple (acer nigrum) are the best for this purpose. Red and silver maple saps have lower sugar content and are less desirable for syrup making.

Acer Saccharum (Sugar Maple Leaves)

Native Reenacting Made Easy

Sugar Making Materials List

- Drill - Hand or battery operated.
- 1 1/2" Drill Bit.
- 1/2" Pipe or tube - 1 for each tree tapped.
- Bucket for collecting sap.
- Large metal pan.
- Heat Source for boiling the sap.
- Thermometer - Must be able to read up to 227 Degrees F.
- One yard of non synthetic filtering material for straining syrup while still hot - Wool is good.
- Containers for the finished syrup - Mason Jars work well.
- Sugar Maple Tree(s)

Tree Tapping Process Details

To obtain the earliest runs of sap, tapping should be completed by the middle of February. Trunk diameter must be 10 inches at 4 feet from the ground.

Step One - Find a spot on the trunk of the tree 2 to 4 feet above the ground.

Step Two - Drill a hole approximately 2 to 2.5 inches deep into the wood and insert a pipe into the tree.

Step Three - Hang a bucket below the pipe to catch the sap. Open buckets need to be covered to keep out foreign materials.

Modern Sap Collection Method

The amount of sap varies from day to day. Normally, a single tap produces from a quart to a gallon of sap per flow, with a seasonal accumulation of 10 to 12 gallons per tap. Collect every two or three days. The amount of sap required to produce a gallon of maple syrup varies, depending on sugar concentration. Sap averages 2 percent sugar which means that 10.75 gallons of sap are required to produce 1 quart of syrup.

Cooking Off The Water

Fill the cooking container (large shallow pan) with sap. Heat the sap to the boiling point, taking care not to scorch the sap. As the water level decreases in the pan, add more sap. Continue this process until the boiling point of the sap begins to rise above the boiling point of water due to super saturated sugar levels.

Boiler used to make syrup by Ronald C. Yochum, Jr.

It may be necessary to skim the surface to remove surface foam and other materials. Finished syrup boils at 219 degrees. Once the desired boiling point has been reached, the syrup is ready for filtering and packaging. Hot syrup should be filtered through a suitable filter of wool to remove suspended particles. After filtering, the syrup is finished and may be converted into maple sugar by further evaporating away water and allowing the residue to fully dry.

Sugar-Making among the Indians in the North
by C. William De La Montagne, 1883

Acquiring Iron Oxide (Rust)

You may think I have lost my mind at this point because I am suggesting that you need rust for your gunpowder recipe. Trust me, the rust is a catalyst that allows you to omit sulfur when combined with sugar. I am not a chemist but I can tell you it does work.

Rust Collection Process Details

Take a cast iron skillet and wash it thoroughly with degreaser to remove the seasoning then be simply set outdoors to rust. Once it has rusted sufficiently you simply scrape off the iron oxide and place it into a container.

Rust Scale on a Chain

NOTE: You can also locate rust on any non-galvanized steel left in the elements such as this rust on a chain.

Michael L. Pitzer

Buying Potassium Nitrate

Lowe's, Wal-Mart and other garden centers sell stump removers that are pure potassium nitrate (KNO3). The two most common brands are Spectracide (100% pure, per the manufacturer's material safety data sheet – MSDS) and Grant's. The stump removers cost about $5.50 USD for one pound.

Lowe's® brand of stump remover is pure KNO3

Buying Charcoal

I really encourage you to make your own charcoal. This is because store bought charcoal will not work as well for gunpowder manufacturing due to being made from hardwood. However, if this is not an option, Lowe's sells a natural charcoal under the brand name "Cowboy". It is 100% natural charred hardwood with no additives. You can also look for technical grade charcoal from art supply stores and chemical supply houses.

Buying Sugar

Purchase granulated or powdered sugar from the grocery store. I have heard of people using using just about any type of sugar imaginable, so do not be afraid to experiment a little.

Buying Iron Oxide (Rust)

Purchase under the chemical name of iron oxide from a chemical supply house or art supply store.

Michael L. Pitzer

Preparing Materials to Make Gunpowder

All of the ingredients must be ground into a very fine powder to make the best quality black powder possible. This can be accomplished using a mortar and pestle or you can cheat and use a coffee grinder (see warning below).

PLEASE NOTE: The coffee grinder route is very dangerous and may cause an explosion. To minimize the potential for accidental fire or explosion, the grinder must be thoroughly cleaned between ingredients and the time should be kept minimal. The author nor publisher accept responsibility for the use or misuse of this information.

Hamilton Beach® brand Coffee Grinder by Dakota S. Pitzer

Gunpowder Materials List

- 16 OZ Potassium Nitrate aka KNO3, saltpeter.
- 16 OZ Charcoal - Softwood & homemade are best.
- 16 OZ Granulated table sugar - Any brand is OK.
- 16 OZ Iron Oxide - Scrape rust from iron.
- Electric Skillet.
- Digital Cooking Scale - Grams.
- Mortar & Pestle.
- Coffee Grinder – Optional.
- Wooden or silicone spoon/spatula.
- Mixing container.
- Cookie Sheet.

Second Gunpowder Recipe

Another recipe of making gunpowder uses sulfur in place of sugar and iron oxide. This basic black powder recipe has 75% potassium nitrate, 15% charcoal, and 10% sulfur. Sulfur can be purchased from the local garden store as a common soil additive.

Michael L. Pitzer

Gunpowder Making Process Details

Step One - Measure out 45 grams of potassium nitrate.

Step Two - Grind or crush it into a very fine powder and then put it into a mixing container with the KNO3.

Mortar & Pestle by Dakota S. Pitzer

Step Three - Measure out 9 grams of charcoal and grind or crush the charcoal into fine powder then put the charcoal into a mixing container with the potassium nitrate and sugar.

Step Four - Now add 1 tablespoon of rust to the other ingredients and mix it together well. Add either water; stale urine or alcohol then stir the ingredients until the color is an even reddish brown throughout.

Step Five - Put the mixture on a hot plate and do not stop stirring as the water simmers off. The mix will begin to thicken and should be removed from the heat when it reaches an oatmeal like consistency.

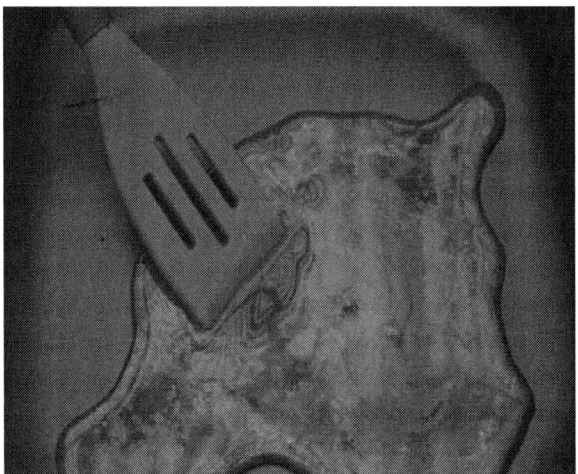

Stirring the Mixture (Low Heat) by Dakota S. Pitzer

Step Six - Put the mixture on a cookie sheet or plate and let it dry thoroughly. After it dries beyond being sticky to the touch, take a knife and cut the powder into progressively smaller chunks. Gently crush it into fine powder in the mortar and pestle. Allow it to thoroughly dry before use.

Michael L. Pitzer

"Your forefathers crossed the great water and landed on this island. Their numbers were small. We took pity on them and they sat down among us. We gave them corn and meat. They gave us poison in return."

Sagoyewatha (Red Jacket), Seneca

Appendix A

18th Century Documentation

Primary Source Document

Treaty of Greeneville (1795) (Transcript)

A treaty of peace between the United States of America, and the tribes of Indians called the Wyandots, Delawares, Shawanees, Ottawas, Chippewas, Pattawatimas, Miamis, Eel Rivers, Weas, Kickapoos, Piankeshaws, and Kaskaskias.

To put an end to a destructive war, to settle all controversies, and to restore harmony and friendly intercourse between the said United States and Indian tribes, Anthony Wayne, major general commanding the army of the United States, and sole commissioner for the good purposes above mentioned, and the said tribes of Indians, by their sachems, chiefs, and warriors, met together at Greeneville, the head quarters of the said army, have agreed on the following articles, which, when ratified by the President, with the advice and consent of the Senate of the United States, shall be binding on them and the said Indian tribes.

Art. 1: Henceforth all hostilities shall cease; peace is hereby established, and shall be perpetual; and a friendly intercourse shall take place between the said United States and Indian tribes.

Art. 2: All prisoners shall, on both sides, be restored. The Indians, prisoners to the United States, shall be immediately set at liberty. The people of the United States, still remaining prisoners among the Indians, shall be delivered up in ninety days from the date hereof, to the general or commanding officer at Greeneville, fort Wayne, or fort Defiance; and ten chiefs of the said tribes shall remain at Greeneville as hostages, until the delivery of the prisoners shall be effected.

Art. 3: The general boundary line between the lands of the United States and the lands of the said Indian tribes, shall begin at the mouth of Cayahoga river, and run thence up the same to the portage, between that and the Tuscarawas branch of the Muskingum, thence down that branch to the crossing place above fort Lawrence, thence westerly to a fork of that branch of the Great Miami river, running into the Ohio, at or near which fork stood Loromie's store, and where commences the portage between the Miami of the Ohio, and St. Mary's river, which is a branch of the Miami which runs into lake Erie; thence a westerly course to fort Recovery, which stands on a branch of the Wabash; thence southwesterly in a direct line to the Ohio, so as to intersect that river opposite the mouth of Kentucke or Cuttawa river. And in consideration of the peace now established; of the goods formerly received from the United States; of those now to be delivered; and of the yearly delivery of goods now stipulated to be made hereafter; and to indemnify the United States for the injuries and expenses they have sustained during the war, the said Indian tribes do hereby cede and relinquish forever, all their claims to the lands lying eastwardly and southwardly of the general boundary line now described: and these lands, or any part of them, shall never hereafter be made a cause or pretence, on the part of the said tribes, or any of them, of war or injury to the United States, or any of the people thereof.

And for the same considerations, and as an evidence of the returning friendship of the said Indian tribes, of their confidence in the United States, and desire to provide for their accommodations, and for that convenient intercourse which will be beneficial to both parties, the said Indian tribes do also cede to the United States the following pieces of land, to wit:

1. One piece of land six miles square, at or near Loromie's store, before mentioned.
2. One piece two miles square, at the head of the navigable water or landing, on the St. Mary's river, near Girty's town.
3. One piece six miles square, at the head of the navigable water of the Auglaize river.
4. One piece six miles square, at the confluence of the Auglaize and Miami rivers, where fort Defiance now stands.
5. One piece six miles square, at or near the confluence of the rivers St. Mary's and St. Joseph's, where fort Wayne now stands, or near it.
6. One piece two miles square, on the Wabash river, at the end of the portage from the Miami of the lake, and about eight miles westward from fort

Wayne.

7. One piece six miles square, at the Ouatanon, or Old Wea towns, on the Wabash river.
8. One piece twelve miles square, at the British fort on the Miami of the lake, at the foot of the rapids.
9. One piece six miles square, at the mouth of the said river, where it empties into the lake.
10. One piece six miles square, upon Sandusky lake, where a fort formerly stood.
11. One piece two miles square, at the lower rapids of Sandusky river.
12. The post of Detroit, and all the land to the north, the west and the south of it, of which the Indian title has been extinguished by gifts or grants to the French or English governments: and so much more land to be annexed to the district of Detroit, as shall be comprehended between the river Rosine, on the south, lake St. Clair on the north, and a line, the general course whereof shall be six miles distant from the west end of lake Erie and Detroit river.
13. The post of Michilimackinac, and all the land on the island on which that post stands, and the main land adjacent, of which the Indian title has been extinguished by gifts or grants to the French or English governments; and a piece of land on the main to the north of the island, to measure six miles, on lake Huron, or the strait between lakes

Huron and Michigan, and to extend three miles back from the water of the lake or strait; and also, the Island De Bois Blanc, being an extra and voluntary gift of the Chippewa nation.

14. One piece of land six miles square, at the mouth of Chikago river, emptying into the southwest end of lake Michigan, where a fort formerly stood.
15. One piece twelve miles square, at or near the mouth of the Illinois river, emptying into the Mississippi.
16. One piece six miles square, at the old Piorias fort and village near the south end of the Illinois lake, on said Illinois river. And whenever the United States shall think proper to survey and mark the boundaries of the lands hereby ceded to them, they shall give timely notice thereof to the said tribes of Indians, that they may appoint some of their wise chiefs to attend and see that the lines are run according to the terms of this treaty.

And the said Indian tribes will allow to the people of the United States a free passage by land and by water, as one and the other shall be found convenient, through their country, along the chain of posts hereinbefore mentioned; that is to say, from the commencement of the portage aforesaid, at or near Loromie's store, thence along said portage to the St. Mary's, and down the same to fort Wayne, and then down the Miami, to lake Erie; again, from the commencement of the portage at or near

Michael L. Pitzer

Loromie's store along the portage from thence to the river Auglaize, and down the same to its junction with the Miami at fort Defiance; again, from the commencement of the portage aforesaid, to Sandusky river, and down the same to Sandusky bay and lake Erie, and from Sandusky to the post which shall be taken at or near the foot of the Rapids of the Miami of the lake; and from thence to Detroit. Again, from the mouth of Chikago, to the commencement of the portage, between that river and the Illinois, and down the Illinois river to the Mississippi; also, from fort Wayne, along the portage aforesaid, which leads to the Wabash, and then down the Wabash to the Ohio. And the said Indian tribes will also allow to the people of the United States, the free use of the harbors and mouths of rivers along the lakes adjoining the Indian lands, for sheltering vessels and boats, and liberty to land their cargoes where necessary for their safety.

Art. 4: In consideration of the peace now established, and of the cessions and relinquishments of lands made in the preceding article by the said tribes of Indians, and to manifest the liberality of the United States, as the great means of rendering this peace strong and perpetual, the United States relinquish their claims to all other Indian lands northward of the river Ohio, eastward of the Mississippi, and westward and southward of the Great Lakes and the waters, uniting them, according to the boundary line agreed on by the United States and the King of Great Britain, in the treaty of peace made between them in the year 1783. But from this relinquishment by the United States, the following tracts of land are explicitly excepted:

Native Reenacting Made Easy

1. The tract on one hundred and fifty thousand acres near the rapids of the river Ohio, which has been assigned to General Clark, for the use of himself and his warriors.
2. The post of St. Vincennes, on the River Wabash, and the lands adjacent, of which the Indian title has been extinguished.
3. The lands at all other places in possession of the French people and other white settlers among them, of which the Indian

   title has been extinguished as mentioned in the 3d article; and
4. The post of fort Massac towards the mouth of the Ohio. To which several parcels of land so excepted, the said tribes relinquish all the title and claim which they or any of them may have.

And for the same considerations and with the same views as above mentioned, the United States now deliver to the said Indian tribes a quantity of goods to the value of twenty thousand dollars, the receipt whereof they do hereby acknowledge; and henceforward every year, forever, the United States will deliver, at some convenient place northward of the river Ohio, like useful goods, suited to the circumstances of the Indians, of the value of nine thousand five hundred dollars; reckoning that value at the first cost of the goods in the city or place in the United States where they shall be procured. The tribes to which those goods are to be annually delivered, and the proportions in which they are to be delivered, are the following:

1. To the Wyandots, the amount of one thousand dollars.
2. To the Delawares, the amount of one thousand dollars.
3. To the Shawanees, the amount of one thousand dollars.
4. To the Miamis, the amount of one thousand dollars.
5. To the Ottawas, the amount of one thousand dollars.
6. To the Chippewas, the amount of one thousand dollars.
7. To the Pattawatimas, the amount of one thousand dollars, and.
8. To the Kickapoo, Wea, Eel River, Piankeshaw, and Kaskaskia tribes, the amount of five hundred dollars each.

Provided, that if either of the said tribes shall hereafter, at an annual delivery of their share of the goods aforesaid, desire that a part of their annuity should be furnished in domestic animals, implements of husbandry, and other utensils convenient for them, and in compensation to useful artificers who may reside with or near them, and be employed for their benefit, the same shall, at the subsequent annual deliveries, be furnished accordingly.

Art. 5: To prevent any misunderstanding about the Indian

lands relinquished by the United States in the fourth article, it is now explicitly declared, that the meaning of that relinquishment is this: the Indian tribes who have a right to those lands, are quietly to enjoy them, hunting, planting, and dwelling thereon, so long as they please, without any molestation from the United States; but when those tribes, or any of them, shall be disposed to sell their lands, or any part of them, they are to be sold only to the United States; and until such sale, the United States will protect all the said Indian tribes in the quiet enjoyment of their lands against all citizens of the United States, and against all other white persons who intrude upon the same. And the said Indian tribes again acknowledge themselves to be under the protection of the said United States, and no other power whatever.

Art. 6: If any citizen of the United States, or any other white person or persons, shall presume to settle upon the lands now relinquished by the United States, such citizen or other person shall be out of the protection of the United States; and the Indian tribe, on whose land the settlement shall be made, may drive off the settler, or punish him in such manner as they shall think fit; and because such settlements, made without the consent of the United States, will be injurious to them as well as to the Indians, the United States shall be at liberty to break them up, and remove and punish the settlers as they shall think proper, and so effect that protection of the Indian lands herein before stipulated.

Art. 7: The said tribes of Indians, parties to this treaty, shall be at liberty to hunt within the territory and lands which they have now ceded to the United States, without hindrance or molestation, so long as they demean themselves peaceably, and offer no injury to the people of the United States.

Art. 8: Trade shall be opened with the said Indian tribes; and they do hereby respectively engage to afford protection to such persons, with their property, as shall be duly licensed to reside among them for the purpose of trade; and to their agents and servants; but no person shall be permitted to reside among them for the purpose of trade; and to their agents and servants; but no person shall be permitted to reside at any of their towns or hunting camps, as a trader, who is not furnished with a license for that purpose, under the hand and seal of the superintendent of the department northwest of the Ohio, or such other person as the President

of the United States shall authorize to grant such licenses; to the end, that the said Indians may not be imposed on in their trade.* And if any licensed trader shall abuse his privilege by unfair dealing, upon complaint and proof thereof, his license shall be taken from him, and he shall be further punished according to the laws of the United States. And if any person shall intrude himself as a trader, without such license, the said Indians shall take and bring him before the superintendent, or his deputy, to be dealt with according to law. And to prevent impositions by forged licenses, the said Indians shall, at lease once a year, give information to the superintendent, or his deputies, on the names of the traders residing among them.

Art. 9: Lest the firm peace and friendship now established, should be interrupted by the misconduct of individuals,

Native Reenacting Made Easy

the United States, and the said Indian tribes agree, that for injuries done by individuals on either side, no private revenge or retaliation shall take place; but instead thereof, complaint shall be made by the party injured, to the other: by the said Indian tribes or any of them, to the President of the United States, or the superintendent by him appointed; and by the superintendent or other person appointed by the President, to the principal chiefs of the said Indian tribes, or of the tribe to which the offender belongs; and such prudent measures shall then be taken as shall be necessary to preserve the said peace and friendship unbroken, until the legislature (or great council) of the United States, shall make other equitable provision in the case, to the satisfaction of both parties. Should any Indian tribes meditate a war against the United States, or either of them, and the same shall come to the knowledge of the before mentioned tribes, or either of them, they do hereby engage to give immediate notice thereof to the general, or officer commanding the troops of the United States, at the nearest post.

And should any tribe, with hostile intentions against the United States, or either of them, attempt to pass through their country, they will endeavor to prevent the same, and in like manner give information of such attempt, to the general, or officer commanding, as soon as possible, that all causes of mistrust and suspicion may be avoided between them and the United States. In like manner, the United States shall give notice to the said Indian tribes of any harm that may be meditated against them, or either of them, that shall come to their knowledge; and do all in their power to hinder and prevent the same, that the friendship between them may be uninterrupted.

Art. 10: All other treaties heretofore made between the United States, and the said Indian tribes, or any of them, since the treaty of 1783, between the United States and Great Britain, that come within the purview of this treaty, shall henceforth cease and become void.

In testimony whereof, the said Anthony Wayne, and the sachems and war chiefs of the before mentioned nations and tribes of Indians, have hereunto set their hands and affixed their seals. Done at Greeneville, in the territory of the United States northwest of the river Ohio, on the third day of August, one thousand seven hundred and ninety five.

WYANDOTS.

Tarhe, or Crane, his x mark L.S. J. Williams, jun. his x mark, L.S. Teyyaghtaw, his x mark, L.S. Haroenyou, or half king's son, his x mark, L.S. Tehaawtorens, his x mark, L.S. Awmeyeeray, his x mark, L.S. Stayetah, his x mark L.S. Shateyyaronyah, or Leather Lips, his x mark, L.S. Daughshuttayah, his x mark L.S. Shaawrunthe, his x mark L.S.

DELAWARES.

Tetabokshke, or Grand Glaize King, his x mark, L.S. Lemantanquis, or Black King, his x mark, L.S. Wabatthoe, his x mark, L.S. Maghpiway, or Red Feather, his x mark, L.S. Kikthawenund, or Anderson, his x mark, L.S. Bukongehelas, his x mark, L.S. Peekeelund, his x mark, L.S. Wellebawkeelund, his x mark, L.S. Peekeetelemund, or Thomas Adams, his x mark, L.S. Kishkopekund, or

Native Reenacting Made Easy

Captain Buffalo, his x mark, L.S. Amenahehan, or Captain Crow, his x mark, L.S. Queshawksey, or George Washington, his x mark, L.S. Weywinquis, or Billy Siscomb, his x mark, L.S. Moses, his x mark, L.S.

SHAWANEES.

Misquacoonacaw, or Red Pole, his x mark, L.S. Cutthewekasaw, or Black Hoof, his x mark, L.S. Kaysewaesekah, his x mark, L.S. Weythapamattha, his x mark, L.S. Nianysmeka, his x mark, L.S. Waytheah, or Long Shanks, his x mark, L.S. Weyapiersenwaw, or Blue Jacket, his x mark, L.S. Nequetaughaw, his x mark, L.S. Hahgoosekaw, or Captain Reed, his x mark, L.S.

OTTAWAS.

Augooshaway, his x mark, L.S. Keenoshameek, his x mark, L.S. La Malice, his x mark, L.S. Machiwetah, his x mark, L.S. Thowonawa, his x mark, L.S. Secaw, his x mark, L.S.

CHIPPEWAS.

Mashipinashiwish, or Bad Bird, his x mark, L.S. Nahshogashe, (from Lake Superior), his x mark, L.S. Kathawasung, his x mark, L.S. Masass, his

x mark, L.S. Nemekass, or Little Thunder, his x mark, L.S. Peshawkay, or Young Ox, his x mark, L.S. Nanguey, his x mark, L.S. Meenedohgeesogh, his x mark, L.S. Peewanshemenogh, his x mark, L.S. Weymegwas, his x mark, L.S. Gobmaatick, his x mark, L.S.

Michael L. Pitzer

OTTAWA.

Chegonickska, an Ottawa from Sandusky, his x mark, L.S.

PATTAWATIMAS OF THE RIVER ST. JOSEPH.

Thupenebu, his x mark, L.S. Nawac, for himself and brother Etsimethe, his x mark, L.S. Nenanseka, his x mark, L.S. Keesass, or Run, his x mark, L.S. Kabamasaw, for himself and brother Chisaugan, his x mark, L.S. Sugganunk, his x mark, L.S. Wapmeme, or White Pigeon, his x mark, L.S. Wacheness, for himself and brother Pedagoshok, his x mark, L.S. Wabshicawnaw, his x mark, L.S. La Chasse, his x mark, L.S. Meshegethenogh, for himself and brother, Wawasek, his x mark, L.S. Hingoswash, his x mark, L.S. Anewasaw, his x mark, L.S. Nawbudgh, his x mark, L.S. Missenogomaw, his x mark, L.S. Waweegshe, his x mark, L.S. Thawme, or Le Blanc, his x mark, L.S. Geeque, for himself and brother Shewinse, his x mark, L.S.

PATTAWATIMAS OF HURON.

Okia, his x mark, L.S. Chamung, his x mark, L.S. Segagewan, his x mark, L.S. Nanawme, for himself and brother A. Gin, his x mark, L.S. Marchand, his x mark, L.S. Wenameac, his x mark, L.S.

MIAMIS.

Nagohquangogh, or Le Gris, his x mark, L.S. Meshekunnoghquoh, or Little Turtle, his x mark, L.S.

MIAMIS AND EEL RIVERS.

Peejeewa, or Richard Ville, his x mark, L.S. Cochkepoghtogh, his x mark, L.S.

Native Reenacting Made Easy

EEL RIVER TRIBE.

Shamekunnesa, or Soldier, his x mark, L.S.

MIAMIS.

Wapamangwa, or the White Loon, his x mark, L.S.

WEAS, FOR THEMSELVES AND THE PIANKESHAWS.

Amacunsa, or Little Beaver, his x mark, L.S. Acoolatha, or Little Fox, his x mark, L.S. Francis, his x mark, L.S.

KICKAPOOS AND KASKASKIAS.

Keeawhah, his x mark, L.S. Nemighka, or Josey Renard, his x mark, L.S. Paikeekanogh, his x mark, L.S.

DELAWARES OF SANDUSKY.

Hawkinpumiska, his x mark, L.S. Peyamawksey, his x mark, L.S. Reyntueco, (of the Six Nations, living at Sandusky), his x mark, L.S.

H. De Butts, first A.D.C. and Sec'ry to Major Gen. Wayne, Wm. H. Harrison, Aid de Camp to Major Gen. Wayne, T. Lewis, Aid de Camp to Major Gen. Wayne, James O'Hara, Quartermaster Gen'l. John Mills, Major of Infantry, and Adj. Gen'l. Caleb Swan, P.M.T.U.S. Gen. Demter, Lieut. Artillery, Vigo, P. Frs. La Fontaine, Ast. Lasselle, Sworn interpreters. H. Lasselle, Wm. Wells, Js. Beau Bien, Jacques Lasselle, David Jones, Chaplain U.S.S. M. Morins, Lewis Beaufait, Bt. Sans Crainte, R. Lachambre, Christopher Miller, Jas. Pepen, Robert Wilson, Baties Coutien, Abraham Williams, his x mark P. Navarre. Isaac Zane, his x mark.

Michael L. Pitzer

Examples of 18th Century Art

Full-length portrait of Tecumseh, Drawn by F. Brigden, ca. 1790-1799 Chief Logan of the Mingo Tribe, Artist & Date Unknown Sketch Ohio Historical Society

Native Reenacting Made Easy

"The Indians giving a talk to Colonel Bouquet in a conference at a council fire, near his camp on the banks of Muskingum in North America in Oct. 1764" Engraving by Grignion after a painting by Benjamin West

Michael L. Pitzer

"Algonquin Couple", an 18th-century watercolor by an unknown artist. Courtesy of the City of Montreal Records Management & Archives, Montreal, Canada

Native Reenacting Made Easy

Delaware Chief 1737 Lapowinsa, Artist Unknown

Michael L. Pitzer

Sauvage de la Nation Kaskaskias Tiré de de La Carte générale du cours de la rivière de l'Ohio, par Joseph Wabun, 1796.

Native Reenacting Made Easy

Sauvage de la Nation des Shawanoes
By Joseph Wabun, 1796

Michael L. Pitzer

Painting by Charles Bird King, According to McKenney and Hall's "History of the Indian Tribes of North America". In 1836, Kishkalwa was between 85 and 90 years old, still the head of the Shawnee nation and living on the Kansas River, in the neighborhood of the Sabine.

Appendix B
Resources

American Pioneer Inc.
P.O. Box 50049
Bowling Green, KY 42102-2649
Phone 800-743-4675
Fax: 270-782-7506
www.americanpioneervideo.com

Several informative videos on 18th century living history. They have videos on gun making, knife making, engraving, relief carving, blacksmithing, etc.

Scurlock Publishing Co., Inc.
1293 Myrtle Springs Road
Texarkana TX 75503
Phone 800-228-6389 (Orders only)
http://store.scurlockpublishing.com/

Good selection of books, DVDs, CDs and patterns related to early American history. Publisher of Muzzleloader Magazine.

Tandy Leather Factory, Inc.
1900 SE Loop 820
Fort Worth, TX 76140
Phone: 817-872-3200
Hours: Monday to Friday, 9 a.m. to 5 p.m. CST
tlfhelp@tandyleather.com

Michael L. Pitzer

They offer just about anything you need in terms of leather craft supplies, tools and native style crafts.

Crazy Crow Trading Post
P.O. Box 847
Pottsboro, TX 75076
Phone 800-786-6210
Fax 903-786-9059
www.crazycrow.com

They offer just about anything you need in terms of Native crafts or supplies.

Track of the Wolf
18308 Joplin Street NW
Elk River, MN 55330-1773
Phone 763-633-2500
Fax 763-633-2550
www.trackofthewolf.com

They have a huge assortment of black powder firearm kits, accessories and living history supplies.

Tiger-Hunt Wood Products
Michael D. Barton
PO Box 379
Beaverdale, PA 15921
814-472-5161
email: TigerHunt4@aol.com

They specialize in stocks and pre-carved ball war clubs.

Native Reenacting Made Easy

Corum Knives & Quill Work
956 E. Washington Street
Greensburg, IN 47240
Phone 812-663-7508

They make high quality knives and nice quill work for a very reasonable price.

Lenape Traditional Tanners
Jim Green
Phone 502-742-7485

Brain tan leather and very good Native crafts for living history interpreters.

The R.E. Davis Company
P.O. Box 752
Perrysburg, OH 43552
Phone: 419-833-1200
www.redaviscompany.com/

They sell muzzleloading firearm components as well as books, videos, & posters related to 18th & early 19th century American frontier history.

Michael L. Pitzer

Cherokee Heritage Museum & Gallery
Dr. R. Michael Abram, Curator
P.O. Box 607
Whittier, NC 28789-0607
Phone 828-497-3211

Authentic Native arts & crafts. Dr. Abrams also has a nice collection of traditional Cherokee artifacts & reproductions.

Fort Boonesborough State Park
4375 Boonesborough Road
Richmond, KY 40475-9316
Phone 859-527-3131
www.parks.ky.gov/Online+Stores/18thCenturyStore/

The 18th Century Store inside the fort provides necessary 18th century goods to reenactors.

Timberline Traders
780 Deauville Drive (Winter Address)
Punta Gorda, FL 33950
Phone 941-639-2152
6192 S. SR 10 (Summer Address)
Knox, IN 46534
Phone 574-772-4359
www.buckskinnerweb.com/moore/timberline.html

Quality clothing and accessories for 18th century living history events. Good quality and fair prices.

Native Reenacting Made Easy

<u>Dixie Gun Works</u>
Gunpowder Lane PO Box 130
Union City, TN 38281
800-238-6785

They have a huge assortment of black powder firearm kits, accessories and living history supplies.

Michael L. Pitzer

Bibliography

Odom, William (2004). "Thoughts on Creating a Persona", Bill's World Buckskinner's Notebook. Retrieved March 5, 2009, from www.buckskinnerweb.com

Ohio Historical Society (2009). "Treaty of Greeneville (1795) (Transcript)" Retrieved April 7, 2009, from www.ohiohistorycentral.org

Alan Gutchess (Copyright Date Unknown). "A Modest Proposal: Some Thoughts on the Authenticity," Retrieved March 20, 2006, from www.home.att.net/~crowdogs/TheEasternFrontier/proposal.htm

Wenning, Scott Hayes. (2000). "Handbook of the Delaware Language, the Oral Tradition of a Native People". Wennawoods Publishing, Lewisburg, PA. ISBN: 1-889037-23-0

Redish, Laura & Lewis, Orrin. (1998 – 2008). "Native Languages of the Americas: Algonquin (Algonkin, Anishnabe, Anishinabe, Anishnabeg)". Retrieved March 21, 2009 from www.native-languages.org

Johnson, Michael & Hook, Richard. (1990). "American Woodland Indians". Osprey Publishing, New York, NY. ISBN: 0-85045-999-0

Hartman, Sheryl, Hudson, Greg, Lee, Joe, & Heath, Ralph. (2000). "Indian Clothing of the Great Lakes: 1740 – 1840". Eagle's View Publishing Co., Liberty, Utah. ISBN: 0-943604-16-8

Southern Indian Department (2004 – 2007). "Guidelines for Basic Equipment used in Native Portrayals". Retrieved April 8, 2009 from www.southernindiandept.org

Hooker, J.D. REV. DR. (2007, July/August). "Grandma's Breakfast and …. Making Grandma's Blackpowder". The Backwoodsman, Volume 28, Number 4, 45 – 46.

Mott, David & Obermeyer, Rick. (Dec. 1990) "Face Painting" Retrieved April 9, 2009 from:

www.nativetech.org

Trusty, Cindy. (Date Unknown). "Top 10 Safety Tips for Face Painting". Retrieved April 9, 2009 from www.painting.bout.com

Michael L. Pitzer

Author Unknown. (1998). "Paint, Dye, and Ink Recipes". Retrieved April 10, 2009 from www.canteach. ca/elementary/recipe1.html

Drimmer , Frederick. (1985). "Captured by the Indians: 15 Firsthand Accounts, 1750-1870" Courier Dover Publications. ISBN 0486249018, 9780486249018

Abbott, John, S.C. (1874). "Daniel Boone: the pioneer of Kentucky" Published by Dodd, Mead, Original from the University of Michigan Digitized Nov 1, 2007

Author Unknown. (Date Unknown) "M15891, Ball-headed club" McCord Museum of Canadian History.

Col. John Johnson. "Specimen of Shawanoese & Wyandott, or Huron Language". Date & Publisher Unknown.

Native Reenacting Made Easy

HOW TO ORDER

Via our website: www.axeheadpublishing.com

Via email: orders@axeheadpublishing.com

U.S. Mail:

Axehead Publishing, LLC
8401 Shelbyville Road, Suite 103
Louisville, KY 40222

Cost: $19.95 USD + $4.00 USD Shipping

Quantity Discounts Available for Distributors

Michael L. Pitzer